MW01601548

THEY SAY I'M SPECIAL

100 tips for raising

A happy & resilient child with special needs

By Frances Vidakovic

1

AUTHOR'S NOTE:

This novel is entirely a work of fiction. Names, characters, places and incidents portrayed in it either are the product of the author's imagination or are used fictitiously, and any resemblance to actual persons, living or dead, events, or locales is entirely coincidental.

THEY SAY I'M SPECIAL

100 tips for raising a happy & resilient child with special needs

Introduction

1. Accept Your Situation

2. Allowed Yourself To Be Inspired

3. Be Honest

4. Let Your Child Know How You Feel

5. Teach Your Child The Real Lessons In Life

6. Tap Into The Resources Offered By Your Community

7. Know Your Rights

8. Build A Support Network For Yourself

9. Seek A Therapist If You Think You Need It

10. Take One Day At A Time

11. Do Not Be Intimidated

12. Remember Time Is Your Friend

13. Recognise That You Are Not Alone

14. Maintain A Positive Outlook

15. Make A Decision About How To Deal With Others

16. Keep Daily Routines As Consistent And Normal As Possible

17. Stop Expecting Everything To Be Perfect

18. You Don't Have To Make Sure Your Child Is Always Happy

19. Be Your Child's Number One Advocate

20. Be Your Child's Champion

21. Teach Your Child To Speak Up

22. See The Good In The Bad

23. Be Optimistic

51. Don't Raise A Spoiled Child

52. Always Tell The Truth

53. Don't Be A Helicopter Mom

54. Give Appropriate Praise

55. Speak To Your Child

56. Keep Your Child Safe

57. Don't Clip Your Child's Wings

58. Explain To Your Child Why Your Values Are Important

59. Have A Gratitude Journal

60. Don't Let Fear Rule Your Life

61. Trust Your Instincts

62. Manage Your Frustrations

63. Help Your Child Manage His Or Her Frustrations

64. Provide Information To Your Child's Class

65. Keep Your Records In A Safe Place

66. Have One Meal Together As A Family Every Day

67. Make An Emergency Sheet

68. Never Forget Who You Are

69. Celebrate Differences

70. Don't Hide Your Child Away

71. Have The Courage To Let Go

72. Think About Your Child's Future

73. Experience The Love Of A Pet

74. Give Your Child Freedom

75. Teach Your Child Something New

76. Dance And Enjoy Music

77. Encourage A Love Of Reading and Books

78. Find Your Escape

BONUS: Seek Encouragement From Others Who Have Prospered Despite All Odds

INTRODUCTION

I should start by saying even though I am many things in life: a wife, a daughter, a sister, a writer and a friend, the one which brings me the most joy is my role as a mother. Like most moms I love my kids with all my heart. I dream of them growing up to be happy and confident individuals and I secretly get teary when they display qualities such as compassion, kindness and resilience. They are tears of pride.

I have two children. My eldest daughter was a textbook baby. Every single milestone noted in the "What to Expect When You Are Expecting" handbook she achieved either before or exactly on time. I should note that back then before baby number two arrived I still worried about things. I worried about whether my daughter was having enough social interaction; I worried about whether I was spoiling her. Even when there was absolutely nothing at all to be concerned about I still found imaginary things to focus on, as though a mother's primary role was to fret and be anxious about their kids.

Then came my second child, a gorgeous baby boy and I quickly learnt what "real" worry was. Real, constructive worry as opposed to the "everything is sort of too perfect so I'll just make something up" kind. Even though his official diagnosis didn't come through until age three (the diagnosis being Charcot Marie Tooth disease, a rare, degenerative, peripheral neuro-muscular disorder) I already had an inkling something was not quite right at birth. The mid-wife immediately noted an anomaly of his limbs and requested a brain ultrasound which took place when my baby was just ten days old. After that nothing was ever the same again. *I was never the same person again.*

7

If you have a child with special needs then you and I are more alike than you may think. Even if your child has a behavioral, cognitive or developmental issue while mine has a physical disability the same truth applies.

We both know fear, panic and sadness. We both have shed tears over having that scary seed planted in the garden of our mind– that things can go wrong with children. Not everyone grows up to be healthy and mobile. Some children get sick and die, others simply never get better.

Whatever your case may be I want you to know **you are not alone**. You may often feel like you are and trust me, at times I have felt that suffocating grasp of isolation too. Even though you feel that way you are not alone. Right now at this very point in time there are millions of moms in the world raising a special needs child. Maybe they are not raising a child with the same disability as mine or your own child's but they are still going through similar stresses, struggles and pain.

In this book I have outlined **100 important tips and coping strategies to consider while raising a child with special needs**. Please note I do not pretend to be an expert on this field by any means, though I do have a degree in psychology and the field experience of raising my own special needs child. These are simply tips that have worked for me. Hopefully a few will also be beneficial to you on this unpredictable, challenging yet always inspirational journey we call life. I wrote this book for you, just as much I did for me.

TIP 1: ACCEPT YOUR SITUATION

God grant me the SERENITY to accept the things I cannot change, the COURAGE to change the things I can and WISDOM to know the difference - The Serenity Prayer.

I think the single most beneficial thing a parent with a special needs child can do is accept their situation. Accepting a situation does NOT mean you are giving up. To the contrary it means you recognise and understand that your current situation – whatever that may be - *is what it is*. Life often doesn't go according to plan and that's okay. Acceptance means you understand this truth and that you are free from denial, leaving you to pursue other avenues to make your situation work.

People all around the world have embraced the Serenity Prayer and I feel like it encompasses the goal of a special-needs parent perfectly. That's because the key to happiness is letting each situation be what it is instead of what you think or wish it should be. At some point you need to let go of what you thought should happen in your life and live in what is happening right now. Sure you might not have planned to have a special needs child but that is what you were gifted with so learn to accept your reality.

Raising a child with any condition, disorder or special need is indeed both a blessing and a challenge. It's a challenge for many obvious reasons – financial, physical and emotional it can have its toll -and yet there is a blessing that comes from overcoming these challenges, from seeing your child prosper and flourish despite all odds.

When something bad happens you have three choices. You can either let it define you, let it destroy you or let it strengthen you. Serenity comes when you trade in your expectations for acceptance. As Shakespeare once said expectation is the root of all heartache so expect nothing and appreciate everything.

9

TIP 2: ALLOW YOURSELF TO BE INSPIRED

Sometimes all you need is an understanding word.

Here are my top ten favorite quotes from individuals who have somehow managed to encapsulate all the emotion and complexities of living with a disability.

1. *You are not obligated to do everything a healthy person does. You are not obligated to be an inspiration. You are not obligated to hide your illness in order to make other people comfortable. You are allowed to know your limits. You are allowed to have bad days. You are allowed to stay in bed if you can't get up to do anything but go to the bathroom. It is not your fault if other people leave you because of your illness. It is not your fault you are sick. You don't have to apologise for something that is out of your control – Unknown.*

2. *The most beautiful people we have known are those who have known defeat, known suffering, known struggle, known loss and have found their way out of the depths. These persons have a sensitivity, appreciation and an understanding of life that fills them with compassion, gentleness, and a deep loving concern. Beautiful people do not just happen. -Elizabeth Kubler Ros.*

3. *Part of the problem with the word "disabilities" is that it immediately suggests an inability to see or hear or walk or do other things that many of us take for granted. But what of people who can't feel? Or talk about their feelings? Or manage their feelings in constructive ways? What of people who aren't able to form close and strong relationships? And people who cannot find fulfilment in their lives or those who have lost hope, who live in disappointment and bitterness and find in life no joy, no love? These, it seems to me, are the real disabilities. - Fred Rogers.*

10

4. *I think that everyone has something about themselves that they feel is their weakness... their 'disability.' And I'm certain we all have one, because I think of a disability as being anything which undermines our belief and confidence in our own abilities. Aimee Mullins*

5. *When you hear the word 'disabled,' people immediately think about people who can't walk or talk or do everything that people take for granted. Now, I take nothing for granted. But I find the real disability is people who can't find joy in life and are bitter. Teri Garr*

6. *Obviously, because of my disability, I need assistance. But I have always tried to overcome the limitations of my condition and lead as full a life as possible. I have travelled the world, from the Antarctic to zero gravity. My advice to other disabled people would be, concentrate on things your disability doesn't prevent you doing well, and don't regret the things it interferes with. Don't be disabled in spirit as well as physically. - Stephen Hawking*

7. *Being challenged in life is inevitable, being defeated is optional. -Roger Crawford*

8. *There are no great people in this world, only great challenges which ordinary people rise to meet. -William Frederick Halsey, Jr.*

9. *Life's challenges are not supposed to paralyze you; they're supposed to help you discover who you are. -Bernice Johnson Reagon*

10. *Limitations live only in our minds – Jamie Paolinetti*

TIP 3: BE HONEST

One of the things I have discovered about special needs parents is that they (we) are a strong, determined and compassionate group of individuals. We would do anything to make our child's life as comfortable and drama-free as possible. We would go as far as walking over hot coals or begging in spite of our pride if it meant that somehow the quality of our child's life would improve. Because of this fortitude we are admired by others who often don't see all the complex emotions waging a war inside our heads.

I'm telling you now it's okay, important and absolutely essential for your well-being to be honest. It's acceptable to say "you know what, I'm tired." We hear parents every day complain about how exhausting parenting is but taking care of a special needs child takes things to a completely new level of fatigue. We really do have so much more on our plates – with hospital and therapy visits and the constant vigilant watching of our children to make sure they don't get hurt or need help.

It's also fine to admit feelings of jealousy that other parents aren't burdened with the same worries we worry about all the time. I used to feel this way a lot when my son was younger (back before faith and acceptance cleared the path of worry for me).

When he was still a toddler it seemed every get-together organised by our playgroup was scheduled to take place at a park. Have I mentioned to you how much I hate parks? I hated them mainly because I was envious of the other moms who got to drink their lattes and chat about fluffy stuff while I was on high-alert duty, watching my son. Needless to say I could never relax, even when my son was having the best time ever under my watchful eye, because deep down I knew this was my future - I would forever be watching and worrying about him, whether from near or afar.

Thankfully I was honest with my friends about my "hate the park because it's such hard work" feelings and as a result our park playdates became regular catch-ups at my home. At home I knew my son was safe and secure and there were no terrible stairs to navigate or equipment he wasn't physically capable of using. For the first time ever I learnt the pure joy of pushing worry out of my mind.

It's okay to admit you sometimes feel scared and alone. I know from firsthand experience it sucks being the only mom with a special needs child, when your heart and soul is bursting with emotions you need to spill before you explode to someone who understands. It's also okay to admit you worry about the future and whether your child will manage to live a full happy life, independently as an adult. Will he find love? Will he secure a job he enjoys? How will he cope if his body breaks down and he is forced to live a life full of pain?

It's okay to feel sad or enraged if they are bullied as a result of their disability, if they are ostracised or their feelings are hurt or if they are left out, even if it isn't intentional. I'm personally terrified about something happening to me because I wonder "who would take care of my child in the same way, with the same love and dedication that I give him?" It's okay to admit you have fears. It's okay to cry. It's okay to scream and be angry. It's okay to admit you are human.

TIP 4: LET YOUR CHILD KNOW HOW YOU FEEL

The funny thing about love is we feel it so deeply and strongly inside but often it doesn't get conveyed in quite the way we hope it will to our children. For example I love my kids to bits but sometimes they annoy or frustrate me (fine, if truth be known this happens way more than *occasionally*).

Every morning I wake up with the best intentions – *yes today will be the day* ,I tell myself, *I will remain sweet and calm and I will not, I repeat WILL NOT raise my voice for any silly reason.* Then some non-silly thing happens - like the kids fight or they take forever to brush their teeth and we are running late and I have what I think is a legitimate reason to yell and turn from Mr Jekyll to Dr Hyde for the few minutes it takes to bring them under control.

But here's the thing – even though I do sometimes lose my cool I still adore my children to bits. And they know this because I tell them OFTEN. I tell them how much I love them and how I think they are unique and wonderful in their own special way.

My children also know it is okay for both parents and kids to sometimes feel angry, tired, frustrated, or sad. Even if they feel these things they will still be loved by me and others because no one is perfect, and everyone makes mistakes. Mistakes are in fact how we learn things – if you are making mistakes it means you are out there doing something, interacting and being alive.

If you are worried your own kids don't know how you really feel about them then TELL THEM and tell them now. You shouldn't have to guess how someone truly feels about you. Say the words out loud or write them down.

Here's what I would say to own kids:

If I could give you one thing in life, it would be the ability to see yourself through my eyes. Only then would you realize how special you are to me.

I love you. I love you. I really love you!

You are perfect to me just the way you are, with all your flaws and all your imperfections...

Oh and in case you didn't believe me the first time, I love you and will love you always, from the moon and back.

TIP 5: TEACH YOUR CHILD

THE REAL LESSONS IN LIFE

Ask yourself now – what is the role of a parent in a child's life? If you give this question some thought you will note that this position involves more than just one line in the job description. For starters we must first and foremost be their provider – we are responsible for taking care of our children's biological needs like providing proper food, fresh air and enough sleep. We must also do our best to protect our children and make sure their environment is safe, nurturing and supportive so they can grow to be healthy. More importantly we should ask ourselves "will they be happy"?

The reality is to our job as a parent is not merely limited to providing food, shelter and protection. We have a greater impact and influence on your children's lives and play a pivotal role in educating them about the world. It in turns shapes their character. We hold within our hands the power to build or deflate a child's self-esteem, encourage or inhibit self-confidence, through example display optimism rather than pessimism. Put simply we have the opportunity to guide them. So don't just teach children how to count, teach children what counts most.

The following values are absolutely indispensable in life:

- Compassion

- Generosity

- Politeness

- Integrity

- Effort

- Trust

- Courage

- Resilience

- Gratitude

- Kindness

- Faith

- Hope

- Responsibility

These can be instilled in your child by displaying the qualities in your own words and actions. Children learn what they see. They follow your example and not your advice. Whether you like it or not your children are watching what you do every day for their living. It's what they do whenever they are in your presence and that's why it's so important you do your best to be a good role model.

CHILDREN LEARN WHAT THEY LIVE

By Dorothy Law Nolte

If a child lives with criticism, he learns to condemn.

If a child lives with hostility, he learns to fight.

If a child lives with fear, he learns to be apprehensive.

If a child lives with pity, he learns to feel sorry for himself.

If a child lives with ridicule, he learns to be shy.

If a child lives with jealousy, he learns what envy is.

If a child lives with shame, he learns to feel guilty.

If a child lives with encouragement, he learns to be confident.

If a child lives with tolerance, he learns to be patient.

If a child lives with praise, he learns to be appreciative.

If a child lives with acceptance, he learns to love.

If a child lives with approval, he learns to like himself.

If a child lives with recognition, he learns that it is good to have a goal.

If a child lives with sharing, he learns about generosity.

If a child lives with honesty and fairness, he learns what truth and justice are.

If a child lives with security, he learns to have faith in himself and in those about him.

If a child lives with friendliness, he learns that the world is a nice place in which to live.

If you live with serenity, your child will live with peace of mind.

So ask yourself, with what is your child living today?

TIP 6: TAP INTO THE RESOURCES OFFERED BY YOUR COMMUNITY

When your child is young the future seems so far away and it's incredibly hard to predict where he or she may be in terms of their health and independence as an adult. When I received my son's diagnosis at the age of three the doctor mentioned the possibility of a wheelchair during his later years. At the time that one word – wheelchair – was enough to have me shedding unstoppable tears. How could my gorgeous boy be forced to rely on a wheelchair? Our doctor wisely recommended we put a request forth for an electric wheelchair at that point as they can take years to process. At the time my son was still mobile and I couldn't imagine his condition degenerating to that point anytime soon.

However they do not call Charcot Marie Tooth disease a degenerative illness for no reason. Just a few weeks before his seventh birthday we received delivery of a sparkly blue power wheelchair. The moment I saw it and all that the wheelchair represented –freedom and independence - it felt like a gift from the heavens. Honestly it could not have come at a better time. My son was by then beginning to tire very quickly after walking short distances and absolutely needed something to help him stay mobile.

I will forever be grateful for the foresight held by his specialist. The future did indeed come way too quickly for me and I suspect I am not the only one who has felt the rapid, shifting of time. The professionals knew before I did the importance of independence for my son. They intuitively predicted how much he would crave and desire freedom. The moment he sat in his wheelchair and took off I could feel a second life being born in him. Finally he could keep up with his friends.

He could escape and explore to all the places he had always wanted to see, without his mom always hovering beside him, holding his hand. In a nutshell he was finally free to be himself, without the limitations of poor mobility.

So I suggest to you to consider all your options. Community Health usually provides a variety of services to the public from respite to support for free or minimal charge and they are there to help people just like YOU -so please do not be afraid to enquire about the resources available. If you aren't sure what's available in your area please ask your doctor to point you in the right direction. For us it worked having my son see a public doctor in a public hospital. He was thereafter noted in the "system" and has since been seen by all the right specialists and offered various resources like physiotherapy, occupational therapy and orthotics for minimal charge.

Also note the Individuals with Disabilities Education Act (IDEA) is a federal law that requires school to serve the educational needs of eligible students with disabilities. As a parent of a special needs child it feels great to know my son's needs are been considered and accommodated for in the educational system. If your child receives special education services he or she will have an IEP (Individualized Education Program) written out which is an important legal document. This document identifies what your child's needs are, the services the school aims to provide and how progress will be measured. It should note any modifications and accommodations that will be provided to help your child make progress, their present level of performance and what your child's annual educational goal is.

There are also various organizations and groups already formed, to help provide support to those in need. So search for them on the internet and Facebook or call and ask around. The sooner you begin taking advantage of the resources available, the happier you will be.

TIP 7: KNOW YOUR RIGHTS

Here in Australia we have the Disability Discrimination Act and the Disability Standards for Education act which both set out the rights of students with disability and how education providers, such as schools and universities, must help students with disability.

The main aim of the Disability Standards for Education act is to give students with disability the same educational opportunities and choices as all other students. Yippee! As a parent of a special needs child we know our children deserve this opportunity and it's great to know there is an act in place to ensure this takes place.

The Disability Standards for Education thankfully protects any person with disability who is enrolled in, has been enrolled in, or who has approached an education provider about enrolling in, a preschool, school, college, university, TAFE or any other organization that educates people. This applies for both public and private schools, any private education and training places, such as private business colleges and organizations that prepare or run training and education programs.

This act says education providers must consult, make reasonable adjustments and get rid of harassment and victimization so a disabled person is not disadvantaged due to their disability. Please note it is not unlawful for a school to discriminate against a child who needs special services or facilities if providing these would impose an unreasonable hardship on the school. This act covers the entire time a person attends the school or education or training course – from the time he or she applies to enrol right up until he or she finishes their schooling, program or course.

This act makes it unlawful to discriminate against a person because of disability at any of the following times:

- when an education provider is deciding what will be taught in a course
- when a person is enrolling in school or a course
- while a person is taking part in school or a course
- if a person needs support services to take part in school or a course
- when a person finishes school or a course
- if a person is suspended or expelled from school or a course
- if a person is harassed or victimized while taking part in school or a course.

If you live outside of Australia please look into the rights that exist for disabled or disadvantaged individuals within your country. I do hope something similar has been agreed for your child as their legal right. Knowing this is the case can help support you in instances where discrimination has taken place.

TIP 8: BUILD A SUPPORT NETWORK FOR YOURSELF

It's hard enough to work and raise a family when your kids are all healthy and relatively normal, but when you add on some kind of disability or disease, it can just be such a burden. Patricia Heaton

Whether we like to admit it or not, having a child with special needs adds an extra layer of stress to our lives that most people with able-bodied and healthy children live without. I'm sure you do a great job at making sure your child has access to all of the emotional support he or she needs but do you do the same for yourself? Remember emotional support is critical for parents with special needs children. We all need to have friends we can turn to in times of need. Friends who we can open up to and admit the truth – that some days things aren't always so great.

I myself have a great support network of friends but I also treasure dearly those that exist outside my normal close-knit circle, those friends who are in a similar situation as me. Though I am yet to meet another parent with a child diagnosed with Charcot Marie Tooth disease I have friends who have children with a variety of other disabilities and though our situations may not be identical these parents intuitively understand the stresses of raising a special needs child.

Consider looking for a support group for parents with special needs children. Even though parents with typically developing children can be fabulous they may not fully understand the scope of the challenges you face. These support groups can offer you not only emotional support but also practical advice and ideas which may make both your life and your child's life easier. If you aren't aware of any local face-to-face groups in your areas please speak to your specialists and they should hopefully be able to point you in the right direction.

TIP 9: SEEK A THERAPIST IF YOU THINK YOU NEED IT

If you feel like you need professional help to deal with your current situation please do not be afraid to seek a therapist. Therapy can provide a valuable source of support and help you develop additional coping strategies to better deal with and process your situation. Remember mental strength is not the ability to stay out of the darkness. It's the ability to sit present in the darkness knowing the light will shine again.

There are lots of ways to get mentally strong and speaking about your honest thoughts and feelings in a safe environment is one of them. There is nothing embarrassing about recognizing you need help and seeking it. So go with your gut feeling – if you think you will benefit from seeing a psychologist who will listen without judgement and give you the space to bare your soul then do it. Make the call. Even if it's one session or a weekly hour dedicated to you and your needs then know you are doing something that will help contribute to your own personal healing.

TIP 10: TAKE ONE DAY AT A TIME

Unfortunately living with a fear of the future can be immobilising but I have found this fear can be kept at bay if you simply learn to take each day one day at a time. I can still remember the day clearly when I first let my tears spill about all the fears I held for my son. *Fear* is a common response when you have a child who struggles in ways most other children do not. At that point my son was still young and I had no idea what the future held for us. Even though fear of the unknown is a common emotion it is harder still to process when that fear involves another human who may not yet have all the skills, wisdom and strength he or she needs to accept challenges in the way you would do so immediately on his or her behalf.

When my son was three I could not picture what his life would be like when he was at middle school, now that he is in middle school the thought of high school makes my stomach clench. It is this uncertainty in the future that is difficult to process: *"How will he cope? Will he be strong enough to accept his struggles with a positive outlook? What can I do to make sure his self-confidence and self-esteem aren't shattered by careless words or insensitive people, who aren't nearly as kind or understanding as his family and current group of friends?"*

I remember sharing these painful thoughts with a cousin of mine whose brother had Down Syndrome. I didn't think there was anything anyone could say to me to make my worries go away but she looked at me and said something I have never forgotten to this day. She said: *"Save your tears for when you really need them. Today your son is a gorgeous and happy kid. He is enjoying preschool and has a wonderful group of teachers who adore him and take care of him well. So there is nothing for you to cry about today. Tomorrow he will have another great day at preschool and in two months' time he will still be enjoying himself there."*

She recommended that I take each day at a time and look no more than one year forward. This meant all I had to make sure what he transitioned well into his next year at school. She insisted it would be easier for me to focus on just one year at a time. So when he was at preschool I didn't allow myself to think or stress about what life might have in store for him in high school or adulthood. I focused on the NOW and you know what, it wasn't at all bad. Life was in fact good.

Living by this "one day, one year at a time" philosophy I found a fabulous mainstream school for my son to start kindergarten at the year after he finished preschool. Once he started there I found everything I thought was going to be a problem was actually not. He transitioned to year one and then year two and year three with the special needs co-ordinator regularly checking in to make sure all his special needs were being taken into consideration (and guess what? They were!).

I have now made a promise to myself to not worry about high school until he is a little bit older though I have already begun casually checking out all the possible options and working out which school will probably be best suited to taking him on board as a student (without any worrying attached to the process). A lot easier to deal with!

TIP 11: DO NOT BE INTIMIDATED

Many special needs parents feel inadequate or intimidated in the presence of people from the medical or educational professions because of their credentials but I urge you not to feel this way. It's important you recognise that these people are here to help you. If you have questions feel throw to ask as many as you need to properly understand a diagnosis or prognosis. You do not have to be embarrassed or apologise for needing clarification or further explanations. You do not need to feel bad about questioning whether a particular stance actually holds true for your child. Remember this is your child you are asking about; you are their biggest advocate and it's important you feel like you can say what needs to be said at any given time.

Don't be concerned that you are being a bother or overly involved or curious. It's important that you learn as much as you can about your child's situation as knowledge is power in this instance. Your knowledge or lack thereof can have a profound effect on your life and on your child's future. Therefore it's important you do everything you can to be clued in on what your child's options, strengths and limitations are, sooner rather than later.

TIP 12: REMEMBER TIME IS YOUR FRIEND

There are some fabulous quotes about the virtues of time.

Time heals many wounds.

Time has a wonderful way of showing us what really matters.

There is never enough time to do everything but there is always enough time to do the most important thing-Brian Tracy.

Time is free but it is priceless. You can't own it but you can use it. You can't keep it but you can spend it. Once you've lost it you can never get it back - Harvey Mackay.

Time is very slow for those who wait. Very fast for those who are scared. Very long for those who lament. Very short for those who celebrate. But for those who love time is eternal. -William Shakespeare.

The way we spend our time defines who we are -Jonathan Estrin.

When we think of time in relation to raising a special needs child the first quote is most particularly poignant because time does heal all wounds, if we allow ourselves to be open to this healing. This does not mean raising a child with special needs will be easy or without it's difficult moments; it does however mean that as time passes a lot of parents will arrive at a warm place called acceptance where these problems no longer feel like a terrible burden (if we ever thought that at all).

Over time we learn to see the blessing within the hardship. We understand time won't make you forget but it will make you grow and understand things better. We learn that time with our family is precious, no matter what form our family comes in. Time will pass anyway so you can either spend it creating the life you want or spend it living a life you don't want, filled with anguish, pain and regret. The choice is yours. Time is now.

TIP 13: RECOGNISE THAT YOU ARE NOT ALONE

Just the fact you are reading this book means you understand that there is at least one more person in the world (me!) raising a special needs child. But we are definitely not alone. According to United Nations Enable approximately 15 per cent of the world's population or an estimated one billion people, currently live with a disability. They are the world's largest minority and in the United States alone there are an estimated 13.5 million children currently living with special health care needs. Obviously this tally doesn't include all the children residing in the other two hundred odd countries but it's fair to say the cumulative total reaches much higher into the millions.

So...the figures are pretty high aren't they? I would have been so happy if only one other person in this world understood my life so anything more than one individual is simply amazing. Just knowing that there are other moms and dads going through similar trials and tribulations makes me feel less isolated and alone. True, I may not have the pleasure of catching up with other special needs parents on a daily basis but it is reassuring to know you are all there, likewise staying strong and doing your best to create a happy and fulfilling life for your children.

We are also blessed to live in a time where there are many online support groups and associations which serve to connect us with others in similar situations. Take advantage of that. Search them out, read their advice, contribute if you have something valuable or even simple to share and ask questions if you need help. It helps me immensely to know my feelings are experienced by so many others in the world so I frequent these groups when I need additional reassurance or to put my mind at ease. Constructive help and feedback is always available to anyone who asks for it because you are most definitely not alone.

TIP 14: MAINTAIN A POSITIVE OUTLOOK

They say a positive attitude is everything and with regards to raising a special needs child I believe that the right attitude will be one of your genuinely valuable tools for dealing with problems. There is honestly always a positive side to whatever is occurring in your life. Positive thoughts generate positive feelings and attract positive experiences in your life. It gives you power over your circumstances instead of your circumstances having power over you. Think about it: the only difference between a good and bad day is the attitude you choose to take on board. A positive attitude brings strength, motivation, energy and the initiative. So train your mind to see the good in every situation.

It helps me immensely to consider this fact even though my child has been diagnosed with a disability because the most part he is a healthy and happy child. He has eyes with which he can see, legs with which he can potter around slowly, ears that hear and a body that can for the most part take in all the wonderful experiences that life has to offer him.

Focusing on these positives diminishes the negatives that come along with his diagnosis and makes life so much easier to deal with. So think positive, be positive and positive things will happen in your life. After all you can't live a positive life with a negative mind.

TIP 15: MAKE A DECISION ABOUT HOW TO DEAL WITH OTHERS

When you first find out that you are raising a child with special needs it is normal to feel saddened by or angry about the way others around you are reacting to you and your child's situation. Other people particularly those close to you like your family may reaction to serious problems in a way that suggests lack of understanding, empathy or a tremendous fear about the unknown. Try not to take their reactions to heart. Understand that some people simply don't know how to behave when they are faced with a child who is different and as a consequence they may act inappropriately. I myself felt this with my parents who were unable to process that they could possibly have a grandchild with a disability. It wasn't fun to deal with especially since I myself was still finding ways to process and accept the situation.

But I soon learnt it was a waste of energy to worry about what other people think. Think about and decide how you are going to deal with the stares and questions. I decided sooner rather than later everyone processes things in their own time and I would give others the benefit of the doubt when it comes to taking in their insensitive reactions. It isn't my job to make others feel better about their lack of understanding nor is there any point in me getting angry or sad about it either.

One of the greatest mental freedoms is not caring about what anyone else thinks of you. Be who you are and say what you feel because those who matter don't mind and those who mind don't matter. Try not to take things personally. Nothing that other people do or say is because of you but rather a projection of their own reality. When you are immune to the opinions and actions of others you save yourself from a lot of needless suffering.

I honestly can't tell you the key to happiness but the key to frustration is caring so much about what other people think and trying to please everyone. So don't allow yourself to be burdened with this additional pressure in life.

TIP 16: KEEP DAILY ROUTINES AS CONSISTENT AND NORMAL AS POSSIBLE

If your life feels complicated or you are not sure with how to proceed with a problem it helps immensely if you simply do whatever it was that you were going to do anyway. Following a daily routine helps produce some consistency and normalcy in your life. There is nothing to be feared about having a routine because routine things are a healthy and requisite part of life. Feel free to plan your days well and schedule the events into your diary: go for a regular walk, prepare breakfast, get the kids ready for school, go to work, cook dinner, read, watch some TV and end each day with a hot bath or cuddle with your family.

The time you enjoy wasting is not wasted time. There is so much magic in knowing that if you have a problem that can't be solved it can sit on the back-burner for a bit while you proceed with carrying out everyday tasks that need to be tended to. Remember answers have a way of coming to you when you least expect it and sometimes the easiest way to solve a problem is to stop participating in the problem, to step away from it and give it some space to settle before you return to it with a clear mind.

A good routine can also be the difference between floating through life haphazardly and actually accomplishing things. With a routine you become more efficient at using your time and a scheduled pattern of activities allows you to know what's coming next. Making your bed, cleaning the house, going to the gym and catching up with friends – these are all routine activities that help you feel productive with your time. Children in particular respond fabulously to structure. A predictable routine gives them security in life because they know what to expect and this familiarity also helps develop self-discipline and a strong sense of control.

We are all creatures of habit and if we actively and consciously build a good daily routine (while making sure to eliminate any bad habits) we will automatically instil good traits in ourselves and our children.

TIP 17: STOP EXPECTING EVERYTHING TO BE PERFECT

You were not made to be perfect. You were made to be authentic. Embrace your real life and find joy in it - Angie Kaffman.

Perfectionism is self-abuse of the highest order - Anne Wilson Schaef.

A lot of us grew up watching The Brady Bunch and The Cleavers and we were led to believe they were the epitome of a perfect family. But guess what? They were fictional families scripted to have every day issues resolved within a thirty minute period. Real life and real families are far from perfect. No family is perfect – we all argue and fight. We stop talking to each other at times. We make mistakes and sometimes say things we don't mean.

A good family is like music – together we hit some high notes and some low notes but it is always a beautiful song. Real families are not perfect but they stand united despite all their imperfections. They appreciate each other and feel accepted and loved within the unit. Having a home to go to each night is a blessing we can never take for granted. In the end they will be there for you during the ups and downs and love you no matter what, all with the knowledge that no human in this world is perfect.

My favourite family rules for my imperfect family:

1. Speak with love.

2. Tell the truth.

3. Forgive freely.

4. Be grateful.

5. Say please and thank you

6. Keep your promises.

7. Share.

8. Do your best.

9. Hug often.

10. Use kind words.

11. Show respect.

12. Be a team player.

13. Make good choices.

14. Help each other out.

15. Be patient.

16. Hug often.

17. Dream Big

18. Laugh and have fun.

19. No whining, yelling or hitting. Ever.

20. Finally, remember you are loved.

TIP 18: YOU DON'T HAVE TO MAKE SURE YOUR CHILD IS ALWAYS HAPPY

When a child struggles with more than his or her fair share of burdens, like most children with special needs do, we have a tendency to want to remove some of that load. And that is fine to do – of course if there's something we can do to help them out we should be kind and supportive. But that does not mean to say we must bend over backwards to make sure every minute of their life is filled with happiness.

- Remember you are not solely responsible for your child's happiness.

- You don't need to control your child as though he is a puppet.

- It's okay to set limits and clearly defined boundaries.

- It's okay to follow through on consequences if your child clearly disobeys or disrespects you and your rules.

- There is nothing wrong with being strict and making tough decisions that are not popular ones.

- Feel free to hold them accountable for their actions.

- You don't need to do anything for your child that he is capable of doing himself.

- Remember if your child is capable of functioning independently in the long term this is something you need to encourage. Start with small stepping stones.

- Just do your best. Be patient. Be kind. But also be firm in your stance.

- We all fear our children will be permanently impacted by experiencing struggle but remember there is nothing wrong with your child experiencing some struggle in his or her life.

- Struggle brings strength. We grow as a result of it. If there is no struggle there is no progress.

TIP 19: BE YOUR CHILD'S NUMBER ONE ADVOCATE

Parenting experts say we should raise children to be independent and self-sufficient but the reality is some kids will always needs a helping hand. When they are still young, they need a voice too – your voice. More than anything your child needs you to fight for the things they desperately need but can't achieve without adult intervention. They need you to speak on their behalf if their own voice can't be heard. They need you to communicate to those who can do something positive and productive about their issues – communicate all their frustrations and desires so their thoughts, dreams and feelings can be addressed taken into consideration. If you don't stand up for your children who then will?

Being an advocate for your child is one of the most important roles you will ever play as a parent. If your child is having difficulties they need to know that their situation and feelings will be heard and respected by others rather than being brushed aside, ignored or dismissed.

To help you become a better advocate for your child:

KNOW YOUR CHILD'S RIGHTS:

Take the time to learn and understand the rights of your child for his or her particular situation. It is important you know exactly what your child is entitled to so that you don't waste people's time or your own sanity asking for things you aren't permitted to receive.

TRY TO BE UNDERSTANDING:

I usually like to give others the benefit of the doubt. I recognise that schools just like people are capable of becoming strained or buckling under pressure so I try to be understanding if they miss something when it comes to supporting the needs of my child. That of course does not mean you shouldn't immediately communicate to the school if your child is suffering for whatever reason but there is more chance of success if you do so from a position of calm and reason rather than attack or anger.

WORK WITH THE SCHOOL RATHER THAN AGAINST THEM:

Following on from the previous point it helps to know that the school is usually ON YOUR SIDE. They want the best for your child, just like you do, but they must also take into consideration all the other students under their care. It therefore helps to be open-minded when you are speaking to the school about options for your child – usually there is more than one way to help a child fit in and be happy. Allow for the possibility of creative alternatives and be open to listening to what they have to say.

ALWAYS BE PREPARED FOR MEETINGS

Meetings regarding your child are an important opportunity for you to ask all the questions on your mind and finally get some answers. So make sure to note everything you are curious, anxious, worried or concerned about down onto paper. You want to use your time wisely as these opportunities to address issues head on are valuable.

TIP 20: BE YOUR CHILD'S CHAMPION

Every child deserves a champion – an adult who will never give up on them, who understands the power of connection and who insists that they become the best that they can possibly be – Rita F. Pierson

It may sound rather over-the-top: being a champion for your child but the term champion here isn't defined in the traditional sense of the word. We usually hear it used as a noun (as a person who has surpassed all rivals in a sporting competition or other contest) but when I say champion in this context I mean it as a verb. To be a champion of something or someone means to vigorously support, protect or defend that individual or cause.

In many respects this may seem similar to being an advocate for your child however I see it as something deeper, something much more than just speaking up for and supporting your child's needs in the outside world. To be a champion for someone means doing it even when there is no one around to see it, doing it at home, even when you are alone together, quietly uplifting and inspiring that other person who needs help to learn how to soar.

Being someone's champion means listening to them talk, listening to their ideas, making them feel heard, accepted, understood, respected and supported. Even if he or she doesn't follow through on their plans, even if they face obstacle after obstacle after obstacle, your constant and patient "championing" of your child will have a positive impact.

Often the difference between feeling defeat and depression versus a serene sense of peace and hope is the supporter we have in our corner, cheering us on to never give up.

So feel free to be a cheerleader for your child – it is amazing how much a person can do when he or she has someone who believes in them, loves them unconditionally and encourages them to never, ever give up.

TIP 21: TEACH YOUR CHILD TO SPEAK UP TOO

As much as it is great for children to know their parents will always have their back there will be unfortunately be times when you aren't there to save the day. Sure life would be great if we could wave a magic wand and watch all their problems disappear with a flick of the hand but the truth is magic wands only work in Harry Potter films. Sooner or later you will appreciate having some time to yourself, you may need to go to work, send your child to school or another activity and if your child runs into a problem then they won't have you there to stick up on his or her behalf. That is why it's so important you teach your child to speak up for himself.

WAYS YOU CAN TEACH YOUR CHILD TO STICK UP FOR HIMSELF

Model confident behavior

Your child learns from watching you so it is important that you model confident behavior. If you feel constantly belittled or pushed around it may be time to change that. Explore ways that you can assert your own needs while being respectful of others.

Teach your child to be assertive

Children need to know they can say something if someone is hurting them, their needs aren't being met or if something doesn't feel right.

Teach your child words and phrases like:

- Please stop that.

- I don't like that.

- I don't want you to call me names.

- You are hurting me.

Being assertive however does NOT mean yelling, hitting, pushing, threatening, fighting or insulting someone back. It does NOT mean whining, fake crying, gossiping, ignoring, avoiding or giving in to be nice. It means being respectful while firmly setting boundaries and using your manners while looking for a win-win situation. More importantly an assertive child understands it is important to report any upsetting incidents to a supportive adult.

Role-play how to handle negative situations like bullying

Often a child knows how to handle a situation in theory but they freeze up when it comes to actually vocalising their discontent. That is why it's great to practice and role-play possible scenarios beforehand. Explain to your child that while he can't control the bully he does have the power to control his own response to the situation. Depending on the words or actions he chooses he can either help diffuse the interaction or aggravate it further. The best strategy is to remain calm, be confident and not attack the other person.

Teach the truth: It's okay to be afraid of bullies. It's okay to ask for help.

Let your child know there is no shame in feeling scared if they are faced with a bully. Feeling scared is a totally normal and natural response. That does not mean however that bullying is EVER acceptable. It is NOT ACCEPTABLE to feel harassed or intimidated by someone who makes you feel bad. Awareness that this is not acceptable behavior or something any individual should ever tolerate is the first and most vital step to assertive behavior. Second is the knowledge that if they can't cope with the situation on their own it's fine to take it to an understanding and caring adult.

If your child gets stuck about what to do here's a simple four step strategy to follow:

1. SAY WHAT YOU SEE

2. SAY HOW YOU FEEL

3. SAY WHAT YOU WANT

4. WALK AWAY

TIP 22: SEE THE GOOD IN THE BAD

I know this is a pet hate for lots of special needs moms. Some people refuse to admit there is any beauty or benefit to giving birth to a child who will always struggle more than others in life. To be honest I agree wholeheartedly that if there was something I could do to take away my kid's pain I would do it in a heartbeat. Then I think about the things that would be missing: how I would have been a completely different person if my son wasn't born with a disability. Because of his disability I truly understand the fragility and preciousness of life. If it weren't for him I wouldn't be a better me.

The way I see it – every life is made up of "good" and "bad things" but they are only considered to be good or bad because thinking makes it so. Life is so much easier when we recognise this fact– that even good things can seem bad if we view it from the dark side just as bad things can seem good if you look on the bright side.

It helps if you train your mind to see the good in every situation. Just like good things don't completely override the terrible moments neither do bad things need to spoil the great things in our life. Negative experiences can actually be valued because of the lessons they bless us with. Sometimes we really do need to experience the bad in order to appreciate the good. So try to look for the good in every bad – after all, it's much better to be grateful rather than hateful.

In the end life is short, fleeting and precious. You don't want to come to the end of your journey only to discover that you wasted too much time and tears worrying, fretting, crying, angry or sad about things that couldn't be changed. So accept that you have to take the good with the bad and try to be happy with your lot. If things are going good, great - enjoy it! If things are going bad don't worry – it won't last forever either. Try to learn from your mistakes and don't regret too much because even if things go wrong life will still go on. Remember we are not given a good life or a bad life. We are given a life and it's up to us to make it good or bad.

TIP 23: BE OPTIMISTIC

A pessimist is one who makes difficulties of his opportunities while an optimist is one who makes opportunities of his difficulties. Harry Truman.

When you have a child with special needs it is up to you to make the best of your situation. You can either choose to be optimistic and hopeful about life or pessimistic and depressed. Can you guess which viewpoint I think would be most beneficial for you to take?

One of my favourite pieces of advice goes as follows:

Watch your thoughts: they become words;

Watch your words: they become actions;

Watch your actions: they become habits;

Watch your habits: they become character;

Watch your character: it becomes your destiny.

That is why I think it is so important to be optimistic – about life, your family, love and the world. I truly think there is magic in optimism. When we think with optimism we experience happiness. Likewise when we think with pessimism we experience life negatively. As Harry Truman noted in the above quote a pessimist sees the difficulty in every opportunity – the optimist sees the opportunity in every difficulty.

So what sort of mood will you choose to be in today? Today you can choose to be in a good mood or in a bad mood - the only difference is your attitude. It helps to remember there is nothing positive to be gained from pessimism. If you expect the worst the worst will often come your way so try not to dwell on the negatives.

Optimism on the other hand is like a happiness magnet. If you do your best to stay optimistic life has a way of rewarding you with positive things. Good people are often drawn to those who radiate love and positivity and it's always great to have more dependable, caring and nurturing friends in your life.

Sure not every day is going to be great but there is something good in every day so find it -seek out the goodness! Those little bursts of sunshine and joy! After all happiness is not the absence of problems. It's the ability to deal with them with a patient heart. Give yourself permission to be positive every day.

TIP 24: TEACH YOUR CHILD TO BE OPTIMISTIC

Nothing can be done without hope and confidence. Helen Keller.

I have already raved about the importance of optimism. Now here are some tips to help you instil the same positive outlook in your child.

WHAT YOU CAN DO TO ENCOURAGE OPTIMISM:

1. Spend time together as a family.

When children feel loved, secure and safe in their home they tend to have a stronger sense of self-confidence and self-esteem. In our family we have opted to have my in-laws (that is, my children's grandparents) live with us in our home as they are such an integral part of our life. They also happen to be great role models for the children. We love having them around and I think their presence has helped show our children through example how important it is for families to stick together, to spend time together and treasure the relationships we have with one another.

2. Be Mindful of what you say

I know it seems like our kids don't listen to us most of the time but the truth is their ears are way bigger than they appear to be.

Whether we realize it or not our children are either consciously or subconsciously taking in every word we say. And when I say everything - yes I do mean even our most careless and critical of words.

So be careful of which words you choose to use. Even when you don't mean to be abrupt or rude or belittling (and that includes words spoken in jest) your child may potentially process your words literally and take them to be the truth. So choose your words wisely and try to speak only kind, positive and encouraging words as this will help develop your child's confidence. When they are confident they have more chance of succeeding.

3. Lead by example

If you are generally happy and don't let little things bug you then there's a good chance your child will learn to do the same. Complain less and laugh more. Live and enjoy life.

4. Encourage mistakes

Unfortunately the reason why most children are afraid to try new things is because they fear failure. However if you don't try something new you can't succeed. It's important children understand that mistakes are all part of the learning curve.

In a nutshell I think it's so important to encourage your children to be optimistic individuals because if they have a positive attitude life will be so much more enjoyable for them. Those who are positive tend to have more fulfilling relationships, have careers they enjoy and find more satisfaction in everyday tasks. It's true that to some extent our children have their own inbuilt preference to be positive or negative in their outlook however it can also be taught. Therefore learn to cultivate and develop a positive attitude in your children.

TIP 25: REMEMBER TO TAKE CARE OF YOURSELF

Balancing work and the needs of your family is demanding enough –at the end of the day it's easy to forget to leave time for yourself but it's essential that you do so. Taking care of your health will help ensure you don't get run down or overly tired. You can do this by eating well each day and taking the time to exercise when you can. Try to also insert some fun and relaxing activities into your day. I personally love to read and after I put the kids to bed at night I like to lay down with a good novel. When I need to talk to friends I make sure to pick up the phone so I can share my thoughts instead of everything building up inside me until I explode like a volcano.

Remember you can't take care of others if you can't take care of yourself. It's not selfish to do these things which ensure your happiness and well-being. Do your best to take care of yourself mentally, spiritually and physically. Surround yourself with people who take care of you as well. Self-love is asking yourself what you need every day and making sure you receive it.

TIP 26: DO WHAT YOU CAN TO BETTER COPE WITH STRESS

Stress is inevitable but thankfully there are little things you can do every day to minimise the impact it has on your life.

1. *Identify what is stressing you the most in life.*

Pinpoint and write a list of all the things that make your blood pressure rise so you can do your best to manage these stressors.

2. *Prepare for tomorrow the night before*

Just as it's essential to have goals in life it is important to have a plan for each day. Jot down important daily to-do tasks and don't wait until the morning to begin thinking about what can be done to action your plan.

3. *Get up 15 minutes earlier every day.*

As the saying goes early to bed and early to rise makes a person healthy, wealthy and wise.

4. *Avoid Caffeine, Alcohol, and Nicotine.*

Reducing your consumption of these substances will have you feeling more clear-headed.

5. Set appointments ahead of time and keep track of them in a diary

It's never fun forgetting you had an important appointment, especially when it takes another six months to get back in.

6. Don't rely on your memory – write it down.

We are humans, not elephants. We occasionally forget so having a paper trail will help jog your memory.

7. Practice preventative maintenance

You don't wait until your car breaks down before having a service. Take care of your family's health in the same way.

8. Set priorities in your life

When asked to name what they value and treasure the most in life most people cite their family and health. Have your life reflect this truth.

9. Say no more often

It's a hard lesson to learn but these two letters can be extremely powerful when you are feeling run-down and overwhelmed.

10. Learn to ask for help

A friend in need is a friend indeed. Give your support network the opportunity to help you out when the situation demands it.

11. Avoid negative people

Negative people are the greatest destroyers of confidence and self-esteem. Surround yourself with people who bring out the best in you. Good things happen when you distance yourself from negative people.

12. Use your time wisely

The trouble is we think we have time. But life is short and time is precious. You can never recover a word after it is said, the moment after it is missed or time after it is gone.

13. Break large tasks into bite size portions

It's all about taking one step at a time.

14. Delegate

You can do anything but not everything.

15. Keep meal times simple

It's important to think about what you feed your family. The food you eat can either be the safest and most powerful form of medicine or the slowest form of poison. Often the healthiest meals take the least time to prepare so take advantage of this fact. Make memories instead. There is something special and uniquely bonding about sitting down with your family and talking about your day over a meal.

16. Make duplicate keys

Even if you never have to use it having a spare set will help set your mind at ease.

17. *Always make copies of important papers*

You never know when you might need them.

18. *Avoid ill-fitting, uncomfortable clothes*

If you aren't comfortable you won't feel comfortable.

19. *Unclutter your life*

A house full of clutter is not nice for anyone to be around. So be ruthless about the stuff you choose to fill your home with. Ask yourself: do I love it? Is it useful or beautiful? Have I used it over the past year? Do I need to keep it for legal reasons? Did I choose to bring it into my life? If I was free from guilt would I still keep it?

20. *Repair anything that doesn't work properly*

Sure if it isn't broke then you don't need to fix it. You do have to however make a choice when you come across something that doesn't quite work anymore: repair or replace it unless you want the broken item to drive you crazy (third choice: simply throw it away).

21. *Anticipate your needs*

To be happy in life you have to learn the difference between what you *want* and what you *need*. Love and support are basic needs – as is having the occasional break. So do your best to incorporate these vital things into your life – it will without a doubt help reduce the stress you feel.

22. *Be prepared for the rainy days*

Don't be surprised when the downpour comes for it will sooner or later. In life there will be good days and there will be bad; with every up there will a down. No human is immune from this so it's always a good idea to have a Plan B.

23. *Get enough sleep*

It's such a catch 22 – lack of sleep is a major cause of stress but it also interrupts our slumber and our ability to feel relaxed enough to drift away. Try to keep yourself active during the day and ensure you are in bed early enough to maximise your chances of rest.

24. *Smile*

Smiling is such a simple act yet immediately healing in times of stress. .

25. *Schedule some fun into every day*

All work and no play will make even the most patient soul feel like a cranky, miserable lout. So make sure to schedule some respite into your day. Some ideas include taking a bath, reading a book, watching a movie, having a massage or listening to your favourite music.

26. *Do something different.*

Say hello to a stranger. Ask a friend for a hug. Look up at the stars. Dance. Whistle a tune. Buy yourself flowers. Have a picnic. Feed the birds. Plant a tree. Write a letter to an old friend. Read a poem. Go to a football game and scream your lungs out. Cook a meal and eat it by candlelight. Whatever you do remember it's fine to try new things out and fail but please don't fail to try.

27. Have the right attitude

The right attitude can turn a negative stress into a positive one. So believe in yourself stop saying negative things to yourself and if you don't like something change it. If you can't change it then it may be time to change your attitude. Remember you always have options.

28. Exercise regularly

There are so many reasons to exercise – it makes you feel confident, helps you get stronger and leaner, helps combat depression and improves your general health. So let exercise be your stress reliever and enjoy the side effects: an increase in energy, boost in productivity, a good mood and improved quality of life.

29. Develop your sense of humor

Honestly life is so much easier with a sense of humor. People with a good sense of humor have a better sense of life and every time you find some humor in a difficult situation you win.

30. Meditate, take a deep breath or just relax

Where there is peace there is no stress, anxiety or doubt so it makes sense to embrace activities that help quieten your mind. Meditation is not about running away from your problems or avoiding the truth. It's about learning to stop – just stop -and embracing the present for what it is, without anger, regret or despair. It's about understanding "*it is what it is*", whilst getting in touch with the silence within your soul and knowing that everything in life has a purpose, without we understand it or not.

TIP 27: UNDERSTAND THE POWER OF WORDS

Words can be used to either inspire or destroy so be cautious of their inherent power. Once they are said they can only be forgiven and not forgotten. Knowing this is true – that words can either hurt or heal – consider using them to help uplift, calm, support or inspire your children.

IN A NUTSHELL THINK BEFORE YOU SPEAK

Are your words:

T RUE?

H ELPFUL?

I NSPIRING?

N ECESSARY?

K IND?

As for your child teach them to think about the words he or she is silently saying to him or herself.

INSTEAD OF:

- I'm terrible at this.
- I give up.
- I don't want to try again.
- This is too hard.
- I will never find a way to work it out.
- Everyone is better at it than me.

THEY COULD TRY THINKING SOMETHING DIFFERENT:

- I will try my best.
- I should be proud of giving it a go.
- I might improve if I keep on trying.
- This is actually fun.
- It's okay to ask for help.

TIP 28: NEVER UNDERESTIMATE THE LITTLE STUFF

Enjoy the little things in life for one day you will look back and realize they were the big things.

Life is in the details, the ongoing small gestures that stay in your mind long after the moment has passed. These are the little dots of joy you connect which makes your life feel full and satisfying. So try not to get tired of doing little things for others, especially your children. Sometimes those little things occupy the biggest part of their hearts.

Little things that bring much love and happiness:

- Having breakfast in bed.

- Cuddling your loved ones.

- Listening to music.

- Dancing.

- Watching a sunrise.

- Seeing a sunset.

- Spring time. Summer time.

- Having a long stretch.

- Taking a much-needed nap.

- Enjoying a hot bath.

- Hugs and kisses.

- The smell of flowers.

- Receiving a thank you.

- Or a sincere apology.

- Smiling at a stranger.

- Having a tickle

- Baking with your family

- Reading a great book

The list goes on and on...

TIP 29: COMMUNICATE TRUST IN YOUR CHILD

You trust your child don't you? If you are like me and deep down have an amazing amount of respect for and trust in your child then it's important that you share and communicate these feelings to him or her. To be trusted is both an honour and blessing. It not only empowers children in ways that make them feel valuable, it also enhances their self-esteem.

So if you trust your child tell them today. "I TRUST YOU" is sometimes an even better compliment than "I LOVE YOU" because you may not always trust the person you love but you always love the person you trust.

TIP 30: BE BRAVE

A ship is safe in harbour but that's not what ships are for

- William G.T. Shedd.

You can never cross the ocean unless you have the courage to lose sight of the shore -Christopher Columbus

When you have a child with special needs there will be lots of times that you are expected to stay strong and be brave, even when your insides are shaking like a bunny in a foxhole. For most people courage is called upon when they stand up to give a public speech or resign from a job they hate but in the realm of special needs it is beckoned for much less common reasons. Being brave to me means not breaking down in front of others when I hear some awful news about my child's diagnosis. It means not being afraid to ask for something that I know he deserves, even though it may require a battle to receive.

Here's the thing about courage though: it is NOT the lack the fear but the ability to move forward in spite of the fear. Courage doesn't mean you don't get afraid – that's impossible, fear is an emotion every human is pre-programmed to feel. It does however mean not allowing the fear to stop or incapacitate you.

Life is not meant to be easy – it is meant to offer all of us challenges. With courage we find the strength to take risks, the fire to get up whenever we have fallen down and the desire to try again tomorrow. Being brave requires you to stay strong when you are feeling weak and learn from your mistakes even when you just can't cope with having another depressing lesson.

Just as it's important for you to be brave it's also a valuable skill for your child to learn too. Aristotle claimed we cannot do anything in this world without courage and to some extent I believe this is true. All of our dreams can come true if we have the courage to pursue them. Courage isn't about having the strength to go on – it's going on even when you don't have the strength. You need to take risks to accomplish anything in life and fortune often favours the brave.

So if you can see your child is feeling scared about things tell him that it's okay. There's nothing wrong with feeling scared but there is something wrong with letting that fear control you. Help your child to eliminate as much fear as possible because that is often what holds people back from reaching their greatest potential.

Of course in the world of a special needs child the term "reaching their potential" may mean something completely different but that's okay. It takes courage to let go of what you cannot change and if you want to know the truth here it is: sometimes courage doesn't roar. Instead it's the quiet voice at the end of the day saying "I don't give up, I will try again tomorrow."

TIP 31: BE HELPFUL

Children with disabilities are like butterflies with a broken wing. They are just as beautiful as all others but they need help to spread their wings. Unknown

The purpose of life is not to be happy. It is to be useful, to be honourable, to be compassionate, to have it make some difference that you have lived and lived well.

Ralph Waldo Emerson.

No one is useless in this world who lightens the burdens of another.

Charles Dickens.

Like me you are probably already helpful and assist your child in so many ways without even thinking too much about it. This is a wonderful thing of course except now I want you to actually think about it. Think about the gift you are bestowing your child and how important your assistance means to his or her life.

There is honestly nothing more beautiful than someone who goes out of their way to make life beautiful for others. If you have the power to make someone happy then do it. Start each day with a grateful heart. Expect nothing and appreciate everything.

When you help your child you are confirming to them that they have your love and support. Try not to mar the experience with impatient sighs, groans or any other action that implies they are a burden to you or that your desire to help isn't coming straight from the heart. If you have to give, choose to give freely and with love. And remember never, ever to discourage anyone who makes continual progress, no matter how slow.

TIP 32: CONSIDER YOUR PROBLEMS A CHALLENGE

Difficulties strengthen the mind, as labor does the body. –Seneca

That which does not kill us makes us stronger. Friedrich Nietzsche.

Attitude is a little thing that makes a big difference – Winston Churchill.

Once upon a time I would have run away from the thought of a challenge but now I know how pertinent challenges are to our growth and livelihood. We don't grow when things are easy. We grow when we have the courage to face our challenges head on and the bigger the challenge the bigger the opportunity is for growth.

They say a life without struggle is a life without success. I know this idea may sound rather suckful especially when you are feeling alone with your pain but stop right now and think about how you have changed as a result of your own personal challenges. I myself can say I am wiser, more mature and appreciative of my life, especially my family and friends –all a direct result of my most challenging experiences.

Sure some of the challenges faced by families with special needs children are rarely fun but they are what make life interesting and meaningful. Working through our problems is what makes us strong and responsible. So the next time you are faced with a difficult problem consider changing the way you look at it. See it as a challenge instead of an annoying, frustrating problem.

Remember difficult times are not set out to destroy you. They are there to test, inspire and strengthen you. Our most challenging times do indeed bring the most empowering lessons because they gift us with the knowledge that we are capable of so much more than we thought we were.

IN A NUTSHELL:

- If it doesn't challenge you, it won't change you.

- All of our past challenges have helped us become who we are today.

- Don't give up. EVER. Even if it seems unfair right now I believe the universe is balanced and every setback bears with it the seed of a comeback.

- Finally difficult roads often lead to beautiful destinations.

TIP 33: TRY TO HAVE A COMPLETE UNDERSTANDING OF YOUR CHILD'S DIAGNOSIS

To some readers this tip may seem quite simple especially if your child's diagnosis is common and much written about – for others, not so much. I myself fall into the second category because Charcot Marie Tooth is so rare (well it's not really rare; in fact it's the most common disease no-one has heard of, affecting one in every 2500 individuals).

The problem with my son's diagnosis is there are so many different strands of CMT and despite much genetic testing he has not tested positive to any one particular strand as yet. This means it's hard for the doctors to predict what his muscle strength and capabilities will be like as an early teen, late teen, adult etcetera.

Having a complete understanding of your child's diagnosis and future prospects makes everything easier to deal with. For us it has meant researching EVERYTHING to do with Charcot Marie Tooth disease – all the possibilities, issues, concerns about this degenerative disability, then hoping for the best while expecting the worst. I know that may sound grim but this attitude has enabled us to better accept his situation because if the worst no longer seems so frightening. Instead it is something we can manage.

My son has recently started participating in wheelchair sports where the younger children are lucky enough to be trained and mentored by older kids and adults in wheelchairs. Even though the older players have different disabilities (such as cerebral palsy, muscular dystrophy and spina bifida) I have gained much from speaking to the parents of these kids, most of whom have experienced smooth and great experiences in high school and college.

These kids provide excellent role models for my son who can see with his own eyes that a physical disability does not necessarily impact future choices. Our research on his disease has answered a lot of "what ifs" and "what then" and for those questions that are still missing an answer we have decided to deal with it when the time comes.

We are definitely not the first family to deal with CMT and we won't be the last. Others have paved the way for us and because of the support made available to us from doctors and the Internet our road ahead will be smoother than the rocky one we imagined it would be. Our goal for the time being is to focus on getting through each day, one step at a time. After all you can't control everything. Sometimes you just need to relax and have faith things will work out. Let go a little and let life happen.

TIP 34: TEACH YOUR CHILD TO DREAM

The future belongs to those who believe in the beauty of their dreams
- Eleanor Roosevelt

They say if your dreams don't scare you they aren't big enough. If that's the case it's safe to say I have big dreams. I have dreams for myself and my family that are so big they scare me, but in a good way because they fuel my days with hope and purpose and a determination to achieve them.

Because you are alive that means you have the ability to dream. You have the ability to make things, do things and whether you realize it or not your potential is practically unlimited. Now before you shrug and say *"As if – I can list one hundred things that limit my potential!"* – I want you to stop and seriously ask yourself this question:

Are your limits self-imposed?

I know it's hard to believe that many people before you have achieved exactly what you want with less resources and ability. But it's true. Whether it is wealth, happiness, freedom, love or power you are after, there is someone out there who achieved this dream with more baggage than the load you are carrying right now.

The same goes for your child. Just because he or she may be limited physically, intellectually or cognitively does not mean he or she doesn't have the capacity to chase their dreams. Success and happiness comes from knowing what your purpose is, the choices you make in life plus the people you choose to surround yourself with – these all have the potential to affect who you are deep inside forever.

So if my son has a dream, however crazy it sounds, there is no reason why he can't do his best to work hard and chase that dream. A dream should fit the owner so if he wants to be a soccer star then there is no reason why my son can't achieve a spot on the Australian Powerchair Football team (affectionately known as the Poweroos). Or if he would prefer to be a YouTube star (yep you guessed it, that's the latest dream of my young son) then he too could feasibly achieve it.

Achieving any dream takes work – this is not just true for special needs kids but for EVERYONE, even you and me and every abled bodied person in your city. So don't assume that your child's disability is going to hold them back. The biggest stumbling block to success is a lack of confidence and fear and our greatest weakness lies in GIVING UP.

So encourage your child to visualize his dream - to think about exactly what it is he wants. What can they do to chase that dream? The more a person visualizes attaining that dream the more confident he or she will become and soon the dream will no longer seem like a distant fantasy but something that is both attainable and within reach.

TIP 35: HELP YOUR CHILD REACH HIS OR HER POTENTIAL

Every child has a different learning style and pace. Each child is unique, not only capable of learning but also capable of succeeding
– Robert John Meehan.

Stop thinking in terms of limitations and start thinking in terms of possibilities.
Terry Josephson.

In the previous tip I encouraged you to teach your child to dream and DREAM BIG if possible. Now it's time to make those dreams happen. Whether you realize it or not your child is capable of things no one can predict. I hope you understand this truth and feel it deep within your soul. Even if your child is not mobile or verbal or doesn't behave in ways that most children behave he or she still has something special to offer our world. I honestly believe this – that we are all here for a reason and that every single person is blessed with a gift that can be shared with others.

Your child is unique and you know him or her better than anyone else on the planet so think about what he or she may need from you or others to reach his or her potential. Move beyond the limits of your mind. Be creative and tap into the infinite resources of the universe.

Remember the possibilities are endless for your child. As a parent we are lucky because we often recognise our child's strengths and gifts however he or she may just see the barriers and roadblocks standing in their way.

To help your child see that he can become more than what he first imagines his potential to be:

1. Set some goals together

An idea is just a dream until you write it down – then it's a goal. Every individual has something they dream about so grab a pen and paper today and ask your child what it is that he or she dreams about. It doesn't matter if it is little stuff to begin with – like walking without falling or catching a ball. Setting a goal is the first step in turning the invisible into the visible.

2. Provide opportunities

The more things they try the more chances they have to discover a hidden talent. So provide your child with opportunities to find these skills and passions. Obviously you may need to be selective about the particular activities you choose as it can be quite stressful for a child to try something they find too difficult. So trust your intuition and find something tailored to the needs of your child.

3. Be Encouraging and Praise your child

If your child finds something he or she is good at and loves to do encourage him or her to follow through and nurture this passion. Let your child know how proud you are of him or her. Your praise means a lot to your child and can help boost him or her, especially when he or she has low confidence.

4. Encourage commitment

When your child finds something he or she loves encourage him or her to stay committed to this goal. Commitment means staying loyal to your goal long after the mood has left you. I know firsthand children have a tendency to give up and only do stuff whenever they feel like it however if they want to succeed in life then commitment is a skill that will reward them hundredfold.

Commitment means finishing what you started even when you don't feel like doing it anymore. Commitment leads to action and every action will bring your child one step closer to achieving his or her potential.

TIP 36: WORRY LESS

I speak all the time about the importance of worrying less but the truth is it's easier said than done. Sometimes my own mind wanders off down dark paths, towards places it shouldn't and I find myself feeling panicked and trapped in a web full of ugly worst-case scenarios.

So why is worrying so bad? Well there are so many reasons. For starters, worrying about something doesn't ever change the outcome. It doesn't stop the bad things from happening but it does stop you from enjoying the good.

Worrying also often creates problems that weren't even there in the first place. Fact: the vast majority of things we worry about DON'T EVEN HAPPEN. Worrying is such a waste of time because it doesn't change anything. All it does is steal your joy. It doesn't empty tomorrow of your troubles, instead it empties today of your strength. It's like praying for something you don't even want. And is that how you want to be spending your precious time?

So heed the words of Shantideva, an eighth century Indian Buddhist monk:

If you can solve your problem, then what is the need of worrying?

If you cannot solve it, then what is the use of worrying?

Or how about the wise Dalai Lama:

If a problem is fixable, if a situation is such that you can do something about it,

Then there is no need to worry.

If it's not fixable, then there is no help in worrying,

There is no benefit in worrying whatsoever.

You can't change yesterday but you can definitely ruin today by worrying about tomorrow.

TIP 37: FORGIVE YOURSELF

Are you human? Yes? Then accept right now that sometimes you will screw things up despite having the best of intentions. You will make mistakes and no amount of torturing yourself will ever change the past. Torturing yourself also won't help you make better choices.

I guess it's now time to be totally honest. Sometimes I get tired. Sometimes I get angry at stupid things. Sometimes I yell and lose my patience and wish I held my tongue. I am far from perfect and yet I think that if I WAS more "perfect" my children would be kinder, more motivated, disciplined and ambitious. Have they suffered as a result of my imperfectness?

Maybe but then again maybe not…

They may not have the perfect Carol Brady for a mom but they do have someone who adores her kids to bits and tries her best every single day, even if her best often falls short of her expectations.

So love yourself, accept your flaws and forgive your previous mistakes. There is no point in punishing yourself for your past errors and faults. You need to accept the situation is over and that you did your best with the tools you had at that given moment before you can move forward. Let go, be kind and forgive yourself. Life is a journey and the past cannot be changed or erased but it can be ACCEPTED.

TIP 38: FORGIVE OTHERS

Forgive others, not because they deserve forgiveness but because you deserve peace – Unknown.

Holding onto anger is like drinking poison and expecting the other person to die – Buddha

Well if you thought it was hard to forgive yourself then be prepared to work that much harder to forgive others. It's hard because when you have a child with special needs and someone's transgression is related to hurting you or your child you already feel so much more fragile than other people.

Maybe they said something insensitive. Maybe they left you out because they thought it would be too hard to accommodate your special needs child. Maybe they were plain rude or ignorant or they showered you with pity rather compassion. Whatever the reason is for your pain or anger I am here to tell you it doesn't make you feel better holding onto those negative feelings.

So why should you forgive others?

For starters we all make mistakes – WE ALL DO - and there is nothing to be gained from holding onto the mistakes like treasures and ruminating on how terrible they are. Throughout life people are going to say or do stupid things to you, they are going to disrespect you, make you angry and drive you crazy. Expect it. Don't be so surprised when it happens.

Forgiving someone doesn't mean you excuse their bad behavior. It doesn't mean you are necessarily going to forget about it either. Forgiveness is an attribute of the strong and something weak people find difficult to do. If you generally find it hard to forgive others remember you aren't doing it for the other person, you are doing it for yourself.

To forgive is to set a prisoner free and realize you were the prisoner all along. It is a gift you give yourself. While resentment makes you feel smaller, forgiveness encourages you to grow way beyond your comfort zone. True forgiveness releases you from a headspace filled with pain and heals you to a point where you can say: Thank you for that experience.

TIP 39: UNDERSTAND THE IMPACT THAT RAISING A SPECIAL NEEDS CHILD HAS ON A RELATIONSHIP

Someone once said to me you should never assume anything because it just makes an ass out of you and me (I love how they pulled the word apart and made a play on its meaning!) so in this tip I will not assume all my readers are necessarily happily married. Some of you may be married but not happily so. Others will be single parents, divorced, widowed or otherwise.

Regardless of your current marital status the simple truth is this: raising children with special needs can severely challenge your marriage or relationship. It can be emotionally and financially draining and add additional stress to what is already a hectic life.

Even still I think it's important for you to make the decision not to allow your child's disability to interfere or destroy your relationship. Though there are lots of challenges that go along with raising a special needs child it is possible to see this challenge as a blessing.

Why?

For starters you are in it together.

Whether you like it or not together you have a special needs child together and research consistently shows the relationship problems that arise from this are caused not so much by the time and effort it takes to attend to your child's needs but rather from the tendency for parents to retreat as a result of this stress.

So talk openly and freely about your feelings, emotions and stresses.

In times of stress we tend to keep everything bottled up inside. We resent that our partner isn't doing as much. We resent that they don't understand our emotions and we sometimes explode over the slightest disagreement.

All of this of NORMAL though – it comes with the territory of raising a special needs child.

Before we move on to talking about what you can do to nurture your relationship I want you to understand that all these complex feelings and stressors are to be expected. Now it's up to you to decide how you are going to deal with it.

TIP 40: NURTURE YOUR RELATIONSHIP, RATHER THAN ALLOWING IT TO CRUMBLE

In order to survive and thrive within your marriage or relationship you must be committed to making it work. In successful marriages couples talk about their feelings – the good, the bad and the ugly.

You need to make a resolute effort to keep the flame of your love alive every day. Spend time together doing things you love. Go out on dates, have a cuddle, go for a walk together, talk – do whatever you can to make it work. As Ursula k. Le Guin once noted love doesn't just sit there like a stone. It has to be made like bread every day, remade all the time, made new again.

Make sure you work together as a team, especially when it comes to sharing the added weight of taking care of a special needs child. I don't use the word "weight" as though it is a bad thing, a burden that you should feel angry or upset about. But it comes with the territory and therefore should be acknowledged and spoken about. Both parties should contribute whatever they can to lighten the load of their partner so that one person does not need to carry the weight on his or her shoulders alone.

Marital partners make an oath to support each other through thick and thin, in good times and in bad, in sickness and in health. For better, for worse, for richer, for poorer. I know it is hard enough for ordinary couples to make their relationship work so it will doubly important that you make sure not to fall into any traps especially if you see them coming.

Try not to blame each other for the bad times. Blaming never resolves anything; to the contrary it is destructive. Instead pick yourself up and do what you can to find solutions to your problems. Successful couples don't wallow in self-pity. Instead they are productive, positive and try to keep everything in perspective.

If you are married it also helps to provide each other with space when it is required – to have a break, to grieve, to stay healthy and happy both physically and mentally. Staying well should in fact be a high priority for you and your partner. Try to also develop a good support network from family and friends, because you don't have to do it all yourself. It's okay to ask for help, especially if it means your marriage will prosper as a result of that additional support.

TIP 41: TAKE CARE OF YOURSELF

It's funny, isn't it, how we are so used to caring for our child and others that we often forget to take care of the most important person: OURSELVES.

The simple fact is you too need and deserve to be cared for - YES YOU! If you are anything like me your whole day revolves around taking care of others. I give and give and give so much that at the end of the day I am so exhausted and depleted of energy and strength, all I can do is crawl into bed at night.

I think it's hard for lots of parents to remember that it's not selfish to love yourself, take care of yourself or to make your happiness a priority. Rather than being self-indulgent it is a form of self-preservation. To care for others you must be able to care for yourself.

Points to heed:

- You are important.

- You are worth it.

- Self-love is asking yourself what you need every day and then making sure you receive it.

- Rest and self-care are IMPORTANT.

- It is nearly impossible to take care of others when you don't take care of yourself.

- You can't give anything of yourself if you feel like an empty vessel.

Ways to take care of yourself:

- Have a break, sit down and rest.

- If it feels wrong, don't do it.

- Don't be a people pleaser.

- Be kind to yourself.

- Stay away from negativity.

- Go out to dinner when you can't be bothered cooking.

- Ask friends or family to help you out.

- Indulge in a massage, a facial or a pedicure.

- Let go of what you can't control.

- Trust your instincts.

- Never give up on your dreams.

- Appreciate how much you do.

- Nourish your soul.

- Remember what it is that makes you feel special and take the time to enjoy it.

IT'S ALSO SUPER IMPORTANT THAT YOU STAY HEALTHY, BOTH PHYSICALLY AND MENTALLY!

- Eat well

- Don't skip breakfast

- Consume lots of fruit and vegetables

- Take your vitamins

- Drink lots of water

- Get eight hours of sleep every night
- Remember your annual physical exams
- Monitor your weight
- Smile often
- Exercise regularly
- Go outside and enjoy the sunshine
- Meditate
- Breathe deeply
- Improve your posture
- Stop smoking
- Cut out sugary food
- Limit your alcohol intake
- Limit soda too
- Floss regularly
- Avoid trigger foods
- Go organic
- Cut down on processed foods
- Reduce stress
- Write in a journal
- Have patience
- Love yourself

TIP 42: STEP OUTSIDE YOUR COMFORT ZONE

Life begins at the end of your comfort zone – Neale Donald Walsch

The sooner you step away from your comfort zone the sooner you'll realize that it really wasn't all that comfortable – Eddie Harris Jr.

They say the real magic happens when you step outside your comfort zone. That everything you ever wanted is one step outside your comfort zone. Sure a comfort zone is a beautiful place but nothing ever grows there. So it would appear that breaking out of your comfort zone is the main pathway to growth.

When I speak about your comfort zone in terms of raising a special needs child I want you to ask yourself right now– is there something new you could try, something different that you haven't already mastered? Are you confined by a tower of walls that you built yourself? Or do you feel comfortable stretching yourself? Are you willing to feel awkward and uncomfortable when you try something new?

If you do the same things every day, things you have already mastered then you will never grow. If you are always afraid to let go of what's comfortable and familiar then you can never be happy. Sometimes those are the very things that are hurting us.

Just imagine what lies beyond the edges of your comfort zone. You can't see it but the thought of reaching this unknown entity or state is terrifying. Terrifying because you can't even begin to imagine all the fabulous things you are capable of. If we did all the things we were capable of we would literally astound ourselves.

TIP 43: TREAT YOUR CHILD WITH SPECIAL NEEDS AS MUCH LIKE YOUR OTHER CHILDREN

If you have a special needs child with siblings you will undoubtedly face some dilemmas along the way. Even though you try to love your children equally the truth is you can't possibly provide for them all in the same way. Some children, like your child with special needs, simply require more of your time, energy and resources. Still it's important that you make sure your other children feel you love them as much as the ones who need you more.

To do this well consider embracing the following tips:

- Make each child feel special. Parents with a special needs child often spend so much time working hard to help their child with a disability feel valued and accepted. This is fine to do, as long as you remember to focus on your other children who may seem to have it easier but in fact need just as much love, reassurance, support and guidance as their siblings with special needs.

- Be as fair as possible with discipline. If you allow your child with special needs to get away with everything while coming down hard on those without a disability you will only breed resentment. Not a fun feeling to have.

- Don't assume your child with special needs is perfect. Even she is capable of doing wrong and acting like she couldn't help it. She may even use the fact of being more "pampered" to her advantage and this is something you would want to avoid.

- Refuse to make excuses for children with special needs. Expect the best behavior from them that they are capable of. If you allow excuses, their siblings will feel you are being unfair.

90

- If your child with special needs is your eldest do not put too many extra responsibilities on your younger children unless you are willing to reward those responsibilities with the privileges they may have earned or they deserve.

- If your child with special needs is younger, allow your older children to have as much of a childhood as possible. Don't rob them of something that you are capable of blessing them with.

- Treat each child as an individual and give each one the value of your undivided individual attention.

- Reassure each child that they are special and important to you. Even if it means spending a few minutes vocalising these words it will help each child remember how much they are both loved and adored.

- Speak regularly to your other children about their feelings about your special needs child. Ask them what they need and want from you and thank them regularly for their understanding and help.

- Some siblings benefit greatly from linking up with other children in a similar situation through workshops, camps and activities organised by disability groups. If you think your own child may benefit from joining such an activity do some research to see if you have something similar available in your area.

- Every now and then reward your children for their good help and positive attitude. It's fine to sometimes each child out on a special "mommy-daughter/son" date and enjoy his or her individual company.

- By giving all your children special one-on-one time it reinforces how important they are to you and the special place they hold within your heart.

TIP 44: TRY TO AVOID FEELING GUILTY

Guilt is to the spirit what pain is to the body - Elder David A. Bednar

It's common for parents of a special needs child to feel guilty for a variety of reasons. We often feel as if we are somehow responsible for passing on a disability to our child. We feel guilty if there are other children in the family who tend to receive less attention. We feel guilty if we have to go to work and spend so much time away from our home and loved ones. We feel guilty when we are less than perfect.

If you feel this way, don't worry – it is normal! Feeling guilt is a common human emotion and implies a sense of responsibility or remorse for some offence, crime or wrong, whether it is real or imagined.

I am here to tell you no amount of guilt can change the past and no amount of worrying can change the future. Life is what it is and there is little benefit to beating yourself up over things that can't be changed. If you have to go to work, your children will respect your contribution to keep the family afloat. If your child with special needs has siblings they all have the potential to accept and prosper from their unique family situation.

Thankfully children who grow up within a special needs family generally learn to adapt to the needs of their household and tend to become nurturing, caring adults. They will survive!

Finally if you feel guilty about your special needs child's condition it is time to let go of that guilt. I myself have often wondered if there was anything I could have done differently to avoid my son's diagnosis.

In addition to his neuro-muscular condition he has quite a few serious anaphylactic allergies. I used to often have flashbacks to all the eggs and hard cheese I consumed whilst I was pregnant. I have asked myself dozens (or maybe hundreds) of times *"did all my indulging lead to his allergies?"* If I had avoided these foods would he now be able to eat everything whether worrying about the fact he might die from consuming something wrong?

Well there's only one answer and it's "I don't know." I ate all the same stuff whilst pregnant with my eldest daughter and she is completely allergy-free. My husband and I also have no history of any neuro-muscular conditions in our family and my son's diagnosis has been explained as a spontaneous mutation. That is he has a condition that arose in an affected person for the first time without any genetic history. It arises naturally and not as a result of exposure to any mutagens which pretty much means there was nothing we could have done about it. So if I was experiencing some level of responsibility about his condition that explanation pretty much let me off the hook.

But let's say there *was* a family history of his condition I still think that feeling guilty about passing it on is non-beneficial. Because if I could go back in time I would still have my child, I would still adore him to bits, I would do nothing different if it means losing out on having him in my life.

I want you to remember that feeling guilty only serves to keep you feeling anxious and confused. You need to move on from these negative feelings and avoid concentrating on some real or imagined wrong that can't be changed. Turn your thoughts to things you want to achieve in your life, things that make you feel happy. Focus today on the good instead of the bad.

TIP 45: CONSIDER USING RESPITE CARE

Each person deserves a day away in which no problems are confronted, no solutions are searched for - Maya Angelou.

I have come to believe that caring for myself is not self-indulgent. Caring for myself is an act of survival - Audre Lord.

Respite care is a short-term care and form of support for a child with a disability and their carer. It gives you the opportunity to tend to your everyday activities or have a break while ensuring that your needs are been supported. This may be for a few hours, an evening, a day or even a few weeks and this service is there to help relieve the stress of being a carer.

I have said it already – caring for someone can be physically and emotionally exhausting and having regular breaks – or respite – can help relieve the stress and exhaustion a carer often feel at times. Carers are at risk of developing mental health issues such as depression and anxiety if they attempt to do everything on their own, especially if it is not physically possible to do so.

So if you are worried about your own mental health or your ability to cope as a carer please consider seeking help. There is plenty of help and support available if you ask for it so do your research. Respite care providers typically undergo specialized training and can adequately take care of children whose needs may range from specific medical care to close supervision.

94

There is nothing embarrassing about asking for help when you need it. So ask your doctor or specialist which organizations offer this type of care in your care and consider whether respite is something that could benefit you and your family. Respite often provides benefits for the person being cared for as they have the opportunity to enjoy new experiences and it provides something to look forward to on a regular basis. In a nutshell it is usually a win-win situation.

TIP 46: KEEP YOUR CHILD PHYSCIALLY CHALLENGED

Warning: exercise has been known to cause health and happiness

It is an undisputed fact that everyone benefits from living a healthy lifestyle. This means kids, teens and adults should all strive for keeping physically and physically fit. Children with special needs in particular benefit from having a balance in all aspects of their life: social, physical, and mental.

If you have a child without a physical disability then it is easier to get them out and moving. They can participate in lots of different sports such as soccer, basketball, tennis or hockey. The options are endless. On the other hand if you have a physically challenged child then their options are not quite so generous. If this is the case for you – as it is in my own personal situation – then it's time to become informed about the different sports your children can become involved in.

It's true that kids with physical disabilities face challenges. Some have limited mobility and/or tire more easily than other kids and teens. So what's the solution?

Look at Video Games That Are Designed for Exercising

Surprisingly IT technology has opened up a whole new realm of possibilities for helping your child with special needs and it gives you the opportunity to exercise right in your home. These video games are great as they have many levels of difficulty so your child can participate in the ones that suit his or her level of ability.

You can find games that focus on strength, endurance, gross motor

96

development, balance, coordination, body awareness and hand-eye coordination So choose a game that fits your child's needs.

Different options include:

- The Wii Fit game

- The Just Dance series

- Wii Sports which includes Tennis, Baseball, Golf and Bowling, all that can be done in the comfort of one's home living room

- The Kinect game series. These include games such as basketball, soccer, bowling, volleyball, table-tennis, golf, skiing and baseball.

If your child finds these are too difficult for his ability consider promoting other activities that involve moving. Some examples include:

- Go outside and collect rocks, leaves, flowers or insects.

- Photography – they can snap away happily at things that are of interest to them.

- Gardening – send them to work outside. Help them plant flowers, herbs or vegetables.

- Circus tricks – help them learn to juggle or balance on a beam.

- Animal watching – give them a pair of binoculars so they can discover new birds, bugs and insects.

- Play catch with a dog.

- Or they can throw a ball back and forth with a friend.

- Wrestle with a friend.

- Fly a kite.

- Use a hula hoop.

- Give them some bubbles to blow.

- Dancing –put on their favourite music and get them to move whichever they please.

- Make soap bubbles and pop them in the air.

- Skip rope

- Play hop-scotch.

- Play hide and seek.

- Go swimming.

- Visit a park and enjoy the play equipment – there are plenty of accessible playgrounds now sprouting up.

- Practice somersaults.

- Have fun on a swing or slide.

I know full well that some of these activities will be suitable for your child and others not so much. Speak to your doctor and physiotherapist about the physical activities they recommend for your child and think would be most suitable for him or her. Most disabilities can be accommodated with adaptive exercise or sport equipment so try to find one that suits your child the best.

Remember too most countries have laws that confirm children with special needs are entitled to participate in organized sports, physical education and recreational programs unless their presence puts them or someone else in danger. Many cities and towns now offer adaptive sports such as basketball, baseball, soccer, softball, swimming, bowling, and tennis so look into these options.

My son personally couldn't participate in regular team sports so we were so excited to discover the junior wheelchair association in our city. He now plays power wheelchair soccer during winter and power wheelchair hockey in spring.

Some of the brain benefits of exercise:

- Increases the production of neurochemicals that promote brain cell repair.
- Increases the blood flow to the brain which promotes alertness and mental focus.
- Improves memory.
- Lengthens attention span.
- Boosts decision making skills.
- Promotes growth of new nerve cells and blood vessels.
- Increases capacity for knowledge.
- Enables complex thinking.
- Develops spatial awareness.
- Improves multi-tasking and planning.

Other benefits include:

- Better muscle strength, coordination, and flexibility.
- Improvement in endurance and better balance, motor skills and body awareness.
- Improvement in behavior and academics.
- Higher self-confidence and ability to build friendships.
- General boost to their quality of life and self-esteem.
- Improved quality of sleep.
- A sense of sense of accomplishment and purpose
- Better ability to cope with stress, anxiety and depression.
- Exercise also has great benefits for mental health. It releases endorphins that make you feel happy.

TIP 47: KEEP YOUR CHILD MENTALLY STIMULATED

While exercise and physical activity is one way to keep your child mentally stimulated it is definitely not the only way. We can do a lot more with our children to keep their little brains active and it doesn't only involve boring math problems. Anything that sparks their curiosity and desire to create, explore or solve problems can be the perfect activity to keep learning and growing as individuals.

Examples include:

1. Reading

I absolutely LOVE reading and I have tried my hardest to pass this passion onto my children. To some extent it hasn't worked because they would always prefer to play with friends or their iPad than nestle down with a good book for a few hours. But I haven't given up and I still insist they spend a small portion of their day reading something that interests them. It took me a while to accept that neither of my kids would ever go gaga over the same books I was obsessed with as a kid (mainly the Nancy Drew and Encyclopedia Brown series) but that's okay. They have found their own more modern set of books that pique their interest (my daughter loves the Twilight series while my son will read anything to do with Minecraft). Reading is to the mind what exercise is to the body and as Dr. Seuss so wisely said:

The more you read, the more things you will know. The more you learn, the more places you'll go.

2. Puzzles

Nothing beats an old-fashioned puzzle. I like to buy inexpensive ones that I can happily give away or trade once we are done with them. Our family has also taken to doing lots of find-a-word games, either in book form or on the iPad, as they are just as mentally stimulating.

3. Board Games

We are a family of board game enthusiasts. Actually scratch that – I alone am the crazy board game enthusiast who has convinced the children that spending time together playing board games is both fun and bonding. They know all they need to do is to get Mom's undivided and instant attention is to pull out Rummikin from the cupboard. Our favourite games includes: Cluedo, Yahtzee, Sequence and Blockus.

4. Card Games

I have included this as a separate activity as card games are typically light and mobile and they can be easily done away from home. I pack card games whenever we are going away on holidays or visiting family and friends. It's the perfect thing to pull out when the kids start to get bored or their eyes seem permanently glued to a screen. Our family favourites include: Uno, Phase 10, Sleeping Queens and Zeus. Also I should point that playing cards is much easier for my son (who has some fine motor issues) now that we have purchased a playing card holder that will hold up all his cards for him. We also have an automatic card shuffler that shuffles the cards quickly and easily. Both were purchased cheaply for under $10 off eBay.

5. Movie-making

This activity is a favourite of mine as I don't take nearly as many videos of my children as I would like to. So instead I send my children off to play with my video-camera and tripod and as soon as they have that equipment in hand I can see the imagination wheels in their brain beginning to whirl.

What sort of movie should we make today? What sort of characters do we need? What's the plan? They love making movies with their friends and it's something they can all be involved in. Even better is coming together at the day of their day to watch the production.

6. Writing

I'm a writer so I love to put pen to paper. Because it brings me so much joy I also try to encourage my children to write too even if it's only for a little bit. I can't say this is a favourite activity of theirs but they do humor when I give them my computer opened up to a new word document and say "surprise me with something!" They also both have journals (which are for the most part empty). Still I think it's good for children to know they have this option when they need another outlet to express their feelings and emotions.

7. Drawing and coloring in

Put a stack of paper along with lots of coloured pencils in front of a child and even the most resistant child will feel tempted to scribble something down. This is another great way for children to vent or express their feelings. There are also no rules when it comes to drawing or colouring in (well some may say it's staying within the lines but we ditched that one rule in our house). We have a box of art stuff sitting in our playroom so if a child feels like drawing or colouring in they are welcome to do it whenever they like. It's simple, cheap and fun and definitely activates their imagination.

TIP 48: PAT YOURSELF ON THE BACK

How often do you pat yourself on the back for all the fabulous things you do? I'm guessing not often enough. There will of course be many times you feel like you have failed but in the heart and mind of your child you are a super mom. You are probably much like me – always trying your hardest to give your family 100% every day. From the moment you wake you probably run yourself ragged getting the kids ready for school or the day ahead, rushing to get food prepared, clothes washed and on their back, keeping the house tidy, scheduling and attending appointments and making sure that everyone stays healthy and happy.

You play so many roles in life: chauffeur, therapist, maid, nurse, wife, daughter, sibling, friend but your most important role is as a mom (or dad). Both moms and dads are strong, smart and crafty. They are passionate, generous and compassionate. They give hope, beauty, power and strength to their child's world. Parents will nurture your children, believe in them, fight for them and do anything for them. For all these things you deserve a massive pat on the back.

TIP 49: RESPECT PARENTING DIFFERENCES

It will become apparent to you as soon as you have children that you and your partner have different methods and styles of raising a child. One partner may be more strict, the other more lenient. One partner may be patient, the other less so (expecting things to be done promptly and efficiently). One may be more fun, the other more structured. One may value academics while the other may think it's the character that counts – raising a child who is generous, kind and warm. Whatever your style I want you to understand there is no right or wrong. You both have something special to offer your child and it's important you learn to play with your strengths and appreciate that both styles can be just fine for raising a child. As long as you love your child and keep their best interests at heart there is no right or wrong way to parent. There are four primary styles of parenting and it may help to identify which style you usually take on.

AUTHORITATIVE

- Child-centred

- Responsive

- Accepting

- High Warmth

- Flexible

- Supportive

- Nurturing

- Affectionate
- Sets boundaries
- Disciplines through guidance
- Open communication

AUTHORITARIAN

- Strict
- Controlling
- Parent-centred
- Low warmth
- Structured
- Defensive
- High expectations
- Punishes rather than disciplines

PERMISSIVE

- Child-centred
- High Warmth
- Nurturing
- Affectionate
- Low control
- Indulgent

- Lenient

- Sets few or inconsistent boundaries

- Takes on the roles of friend rather than parent

NEGLECTFUL

- Uninvolved

- Indifferent

- Emotionally detached

- Low Warmth

- Passive

- Distant

- Sets inconsistent or no boundaries

- Little interaction

If you feel like you or partner may occasionally veer towards a style you are not particularly proud of (like me for example - I like to think I am always authoritative but the truth is sometimes I am strict and on other days I am entirely opposite and show signs of permissiveness) then that's okay. Just do your best to parent in a style you feel is giving your child the highest chance of succeeding in life and which nurtures best their self-esteem and confidence.

There is no one perfect way to be a good mother or father because every situation is unique and every parent has different challenges, skills and abilities. Simply do your best and learn to appreciate these differences because deep in the core of your heart you know you both love your children deeply.

TIP 50: IT'S OKAY TO LOSE IT SOMETIMES

Yes, it's okay to lose it sometimes. This is totally normal as we all have moments where we feel pushed to the brink and drop the ball sometimes. You have to remember that when it comes to parenting there's no such thing as perfection. So if you are striving for it you have set yourself an unrealistic goal. Even the best parents are prone to losing control sometimes and overreacting in times of stress. We have all have moments when our frustration levels go straight through the roof and our response to a particular situation is not one of our finest moments.

It helps to know why we overreact on occasions and feel so intensely in certain situations. Because once we have this knowledge in hand we can try to alter our behavior and do what we can to improve our all-important relationship with our children. Want a tip? The more we are able to limit our outbursts and the more we can stay in control during times of stress the better the chance our children have of growing into emotionally stable and healthy adults.

Many of our most intense reactions are triggered by feelings from our own childhood. Some of you may already see this pattern – your parents reacted in a particular way (for example, they lost their temper with you) so you too are consequently sometimes short with your own children. Or they ignored you when they were angry so shutting down is a method you can't help but also employ.

Even though it's normal to sometimes lose it in moments of stress it's important for us to learn not to project our past onto our children. We should aim to parent in a way we know feels RIGHT instead of WRONG.

Some tips to consider when you are having an "I'm about to really lose it" moment:

- Press the imaginary pause button and take deep breaths

- Separate yourself from your child until you have calmed down

- Do your best to repair the damage caused by our explosive outburst

- Sincerely apologise for your behavior

- Address the situation directly instead of pretending it didn't happen

- Look at why you lose your temper. Identify the triggers

- Find new ways to communicate with your child instead of following non-constructive patterns

- Walk away next time if you need to

- Choose your battles

- Find support

Most of all I want you to be kind yourself. Don't beat yourself up if you have lost your temper. Whether you lose your temper once or a hundred times acknowledge that you have made a mistake and are committed to doing better in the future. After all you aren't perfect - you are human and there's a good chance you will err again. Forgive yourself when you aren't doing your best and praise yourself when you find you are doing something right.

TIP 51: DON'T RAISE A SPOILED CHILD

It's not what you do for your children but what you have taught them to do for themselves that will make them successful human beings. Anna Landers.

A child who is allowed to be disrespectful to his parents will not have true respect for anyone. Billy Graham.

If you think it is impossible to raise a spoiled child with special needs think again. They have as much chance of growing up to be obnoxious, ungrateful, selfish, and unkind as other children. I know we sometimes have a tendency to be more lenient with our special needs kids. We think "life's tough enough for them already" so we let them get away with things that ordinarily would be disciplined. This is fine ON THE ODD OCCASION however we need to be cautious about over-indulging their every need.

Here's how to tell the difference between a spoiled child and an unspoiled child:

UNSPOILED CHILDREN

- Make decisions

- Do what they can for themselves

- Like to co-operate and participate

- Know what's expected

- Take ownership of their problems

- Work towards goals

- Manage their frustration well

SPOILED CHILDREN

- Blame others

- Make excuses

- Feel incompetent

- Think the whole world revolves around them

- Don't know how to ask for help

- Feel like they don't have to work or contribute

- Ask and expect everything to be granted to them

- Feel like they entitled to privileges

If you give your child with special needs EVERYTHING he or she wants you run the risk of making him or her both demanding and ungrateful. You shouldn't have to beg your child to do things. He shouldn't ignore you. She shouldn't insist you drop everything to do exactly what she wants RIGHT NOW. You shouldn't have to bribe your child either. If your child throws tantrums often, if he or she is never satisfied or helpful, tries to control adults and frequently embarrasses you in public there is a chance your child is spoiled.
So if you have made the mistake of spoiling your child (and don't worry I think my own kids are slightly indulged too!) know there is hope.

TIPS ON HOW TO UNSPOIL A SPOILED CHILD:

Take into account his or her age and disability.

It's important you take into account these two factors when considering what your child is capable of doing. Children who need help putting on their shoes because physically they aren't capable of doing it themselves aren't being spoiled if they ask for help. But if they scream down the house demanding that you do it for them RIGHT NOW I've got bad news for you and it begins with S and ends with D. Yep, you guessed it – it spells SPOILED.

Identify the spoiled behavior

Does your child never say please or thank you? Does she hound you even after you have said no? Does he expect to receive whatever he wants even if he hasn't earned the privilege? Think about the particular behaviors that need to be changed.

Work out if you are actually contributing to the behavior

As a special needs parent I know there's a chance you sometimes give in when you know you shouldn't. Maybe you think you are being too mean when you set a rule so you go back and change it. Maybe you buy him random presents even though it isn't tied to anything special like his birthday or Christmas. Think about how you may be contributing to your child's spoiled behavior.

Make a deal

If your child asks for something it's fine to ask him or her to do something for you first. If he wants to watch TV instead of switching it straight on make sure he has done his homework first. If she wants to have special treat make sure she has washed her hands and eaten something healthy first. It's important you teach your child that special things or privileges are not automatically given but earned.

It's okay to say no every once in a while

You aren't a terrible parent if you say no every time the situation calls for it. It's fine to say no to iPad use if your child needs to be getting ready for bed. It's fine to say no to a toy purchase when she already has a dozen similar Barbies at home. If the right thing to do is to say no then just say NO!

Set appropriate consequences and always follow through

Sometimes loving your child means setting limits, giving consequences and saying no. That is your job as a parent – to give your child the roots of responsibility and the rings of independence. Be kind yet firm and consistent and you will earn their respect.

Finally be generous with your time and love

After all too much love never spoiled children. Children become spoiled when we substitute "presents" for "presence".

TIP 52: ALWAYS TELL THE TRUTH

Love people enough to tell them the truth and respect them enough to trust that they can handle it – Yanla.

Be honest with your kids. Because you see your past in their eyes and they see the future in yours– Nishan Panwar.

Sometimes the truth hurts and sometimes it feels real good – Henry Rollins.

I should start by making a case for why it's so important to be honest. Being honest means choosing not to lie, steal, cheat or deceive others in any way. It means speaking the truth and acting in a way you know is the right thing to do. When we act with honesty we build a strength of character within ourselves that allows not only our family but others to feel at peace and trusted by our presence. They say honesty is the best policy and I agree with this saying. Sure telling the truth may hurt for a little while but a lie hurts forever.

So how does honesty apply to the task of raising a child with special needs? I will use my own family as an example. My son was born with a neuro-muscular disability and his diagnosis has the gut-wrenching characteristic of being degenerative. For years my son never asked questions, assuming his legs weren't strong simply because he was still young and that over time they would gain more strength. As a preschooler he thought sooner or later he would be able to run and do everything that other children managed to do with ease.

The truth however was to the contrary. I can still remember the day he asked me "so tell me, am I going to have CMT when I grow up?" The answer to this question was of course yes -unfortunately a genetic condition doesn't just disappear with time or age. I had to make a choice at that moment – did I tell him what he wanted to hear (*of course your legs will get stronger and not weaker over time*) or did I tell him the truth?

I opted for the latter and gave myself the permission to tell him the truth, however unpretty it was, because ultimately I knew it was the right thing to do. I admitted his CMT would never disappear – it was a condition he would have for life but we would learn to deal with it and manage it in the best way we knew how.

Often when your child asks you a question it's because he or she already knows the answer. This is why it's so important to tell them the truth. You owe it to your child to present the information they are requesting in an honest and concise manner while maintaining a positive attitude.

Honesty is valuable because without honesty there is no trust. Without trust there is no strong backbone or foundation to a family. Honesty is always the best policy because no matter how great you think you are at hiding the truth it will eventually come out. Lying, even when you think you are doing the right or noble thing, hurts the people you love the most.

There's a saying - *the truth will set you free while what you hide will destroy you* so take the weight off your shoulders and be honest today. You owe it to yourself and your family.

While we are on the topic of honesty here are some simple ways to teach your kids to be honest:

- Talk to your children about how much you value honesty.

- Set a good example by always telling the truth. If you are dishonest you give others a valid reason not to trust you.

- Expect truthfulness in return.

- Help them distinguish between reality and wishful thinking.

- Use a problem-solving approach with poor choices. Don't overreact to mistakes.

- When your child does something wrong describe what you see and ask your child to make amends. Give him or her appropriate consequences.

- Point out the downside to dishonesty. Teach your child why lying doesn't work.

- Don't label a child who lies. Often parental labels can become a self-fulfilling prophecy.

- Avoid asking questions that set your child up to lie. Don't ask questions you already know the answer to.

- If you catch your child lying correct the behavior. Don't allow her to think she's getting away with it. Let her know you are disappointed.

- Reward the truth. Provide positive reinforcements for honesty.

TIP 53: DON'T BE A HELICOPTER MOM

It is the responsibility of every parent to ensure their children are prepared for the adult world and that they throw open the doors at eighteen and walk into their lives with confidence and enthusiasm. Vicki Hoefie.

Helicopter parents deprive their children of learning natural consequences for their behavior. Mike Gurr.

Wise parents prepare their children to get along without them. Larry Y. Wilson.

Helicopter mom is a term for a parent who pays extremely close attention to her children and their experiences and problems, particularly at educational institutions. They are named this because they behave much like a helicopter – hovering closely overhead, rarely out of reach whether their children need them or not.

Although the term seems to date as far back as 1969 when it was first mentioned in a bestselling book *Between Parent & Teenager* by Dr. Haim Ginott it only gained widespread notoriety when American college administrators began using it in early 2000s. By this point the Millennial Generation were reaching college age and their Generation X parents soon earned this tag for practices such as calling their children each morning to wake them for class or calling college professors to complain about the grades their children had received.

Here are a few of the traits of a helicopter mom:

- Hovers

- Corrects

- Helps

- Prompts

- Aids

- Enables

- Makes Excuses for

- Pays for

- Washes for

- Plans for

- Nags

- Reminds

- Organises

- Demands

- Micro-manages

- Preps

- Cleans

- The lists goes on and on

In some respects being a helicopter parent may not seem like such a bad thing, especially when you take a child's special needs into consideration. I mean most of the time we hover close by just to make sure our children stay safe. We need to make sure their needs are taken care of and that they don't get hurt. We should be aware however that such tasks can be achieved without nabbing the tag of a helicopter mom.

What's the difference between normal caring and assistance and "helicopter parenting?

Helicopter parents are a distinct group of their own, moms and dads who are intimately and often intricately involved in the parenting of their children. They will do anything to prevent any harm and failure befalling the lives of their kids.

Healthy parenting involves having a different sort of attitude. It means accepting we cannot control every realm of our children's world. It means understanding the importance of preparing our kids to take care of themselves. Of course there will be some kids who will never physically be able to sew a button or cook a hot meal but there will be other things that are ABLE to master and it's these independent skills we should be encouraging them to achieve.

To do this successfully you have to allow your children to fail sometimes. There is something admirable about a child who knows how to pick himself up off the floor, dust off his knees and start again. Long term there is nothing good to be gained from bubble-wrapping a child from the world. So let your child do what he is capable of doing. If he can play safely in the backyard with a friend without your constant monitoring then step away for a bit. If she can do her homework without you constantly having to guide her give her that freedom – even if her work is less than perfect at least it is HER work and her work alone.

Trust that world will reward your child with more confidence, independence and a higher self-esteem if he or she is non-helicopter-parented. Studies have found helicopter-parenting can make children feel less competent in dealing with the stresses of life, lead to higher levels of child anxiety and depression and also a greater sense of entitlement.

So allow your child to do tasks she is PHYSICALLY and MENTALLY capable of doing. It's okay if they struggle a bit in their journey to mastering the task. But if you constantly do everything for your child you are preventing him from mastering these skills himself and depriving him of a golden opportunity to learn, succeed and thrive.

TIP 54: GIVE APPROPRIATE PRAISE

What you praise you increase. Catherine Ponder.

The more you praise and celebrate your life, the more there is to celebrate.

Praising and rewarding children for their behavior is often used to increase a child's motivation. Praising is actually a powerful tool for changing and improving the behavior of your child, especially when it is done effectively. It is most effective when it is specific and when caregivers are mindful of how often and when they praise. To praise effectively you need to focus specifically on the action made; it needs to also be genuine and contingent on positive behavior.

You can use effective praise frequently to reinforce new skills. Every time a child uses a skill correctly it is worthy of effective praise. It may even help if you think of it in terms of acknowledgement and encouragement rather than praise.

Some examples of effective praise include:

"You have been trying really hard to learn to tie your shoelaces. Congratulations for not giving up."

"I noticed you were been particularly kind to your sister today. I'm sure she appreciated your help."

"Thank you for listening to what I was saying without interrupting."

"You are being really patient waiting in line."

"You worked hard studying for your maths test and your grades are up as a consequence."

"You gave a lot of details and organized your thoughts well in this essay."

"You put away your toys so nicely."

Non-specific praise includes:

- *Great work.*

- *Good girl or good boy.*

- *Well done.*

- *You are so fantastic.*

Other points to remember:

1. Understand that motivation is what drives us to act in order to achieve our goals.

2. When we are praised effectively we feel good about ourselves and our efforts.

3. It's okay to praise often if your child is worthy of that specific and genuine praise.

4. Find a way to praise sincerely and accurately.

5. Children remain more engaged in activities when their parents help them achieve the goal, if that help is sincerely needed.

As a parent of a special needs child I think I am particularly conscious of developing healthy self-esteem and confidence in my child. I want my son to grow up to be healthy and happy and you too most likely feel the same. So we should look for ways to praise our kids often and generously. However do be careful because praising a child ineffectively can actually backfire as it potentially confuses a child. Make sure you give thought to how you praise your child so it is both genuine AND effective.

TIP 55: SPEAK TO YOUR CHILD

A single conversation with a wise man is worth a month's study of books. Chinese proverb.

The way we talk to our children becomes their inner voice. Peggy O'Mara.

Listen earnestly to anything that your children want to tell you, no matter what. If you don't listen eagerly to the little stuff when they are little they won't tell you the big stuff when they are big, because to them all it has always been the big stuff. Catherine M. Wallace.

I know it seems like a crazy tip – of course you speak to your child. You probably speak to him or her more often and for way longer than most other parents do. But what types of conversations are having with your child – are they deep or shallow? Are they one-way or mutually satisfying? Do you talk more or take the time to listen?

Be brave enough today to start a conversation that matters. You can do this by letting your child know his or her thoughts, feelings and ideas are important to you. Feel free to start a conversation of your own or if you need some help or ideas peruse my enormous list of 300 questions below.

They cover so many different aspects of a child's life – like family and friends, likes and dislikes, their current reality and dreams. Pick the questions you feel most comfortable or intrigued about and ask away. You may be surprised to discover how little or well you know your own child.

300 QUESTIONS TO ASK YOUR KIDS

1. Name five interesting things about you.
2. Name five words to describe you.
3. If you could have any superpower what would it be and why?
4. What is your earliest memory?
5. What is your favourite memory?
6. What is your worst memory?
7. If you were invisible where would you go and what would you go?
8. What is your favourite food?
9. What is your worst food?
10. What is your favourite TV show?
11. What is your favourite movie?
12. What is your favourite song?
13. Who is your favourite teacher?
14. What is your favourite colour?
15. What is your favourite animal?
16. Who is your favourite person?
17. What scares you the most and why?
18. What makes you feel better and why?
19. What do you want to be when you grow up?
20. How many kids would you like to have?
21. What would you like to name them?
22. Where would you like to live?
23. What places would you like to visit?

24. What sort of boyfriend/girlfriend would you like to have?

25. What makes someone a good wife?

26. What makes someone a good husband?

27. How old would you like to be when you get married?

28. Name three words that best describes our family.

29. What's the best thing about been in our family?

30. If you could change anything about our family what would it be?

31. Who is your best friend and why?

32. Has anyone ever been mean to you?

33. Has anyone ever been extra nice to you?

34. Are you popular? Why or why not?

35. What did you do today?

36. What was your favourite part of the day?

37. What was your worst part of the day?

38. Who do you miss?

39. What do you like to do for fun?

40. Do you like sports?

41. If so what's your favourite?

42. If you had a team what would you name it?

43. What games do you like to play?

44. Do you like to dance?

45. Do you like to sing?

46. What do you love the most?

47. What do you hate the most?

48. If you could do anything you wanted today what would you do?

49. What's the best thing that has ever happened to you?

50. What's the worst thing that has ever happened to you?

51. What can you teach others?

52. If you could travel back in time where would you go?

53. If you could go into the future how far would you go?

54. What do you think your life will be like in the future?

55. If you could grow up to be famous what would you like to be famous for?

56. If you could change the world what would you do?

57. How can you help someone today?

58. If you could make one rule that everyone in the world had to follow what would that rule be?

59. What does it mean to be happy?

60. What does it mean to be sad?

61. What does it mean to be jealous?

62. What does it mean to be angry?

63. What is disappointment?

64. Is there anyone you are jealous of?

65. Do you think anyone is ever jealous of you?

66. What does it mean to be a good friend?

67. What does it mean to be a bad friend?

68. Do you know anyone who is always happy?

69. Is there anything you are scared of?

70. What am I like as a parent?

71. What can you do to improve yourself?

72. What can I do to improve myself?

73. Have you ever been embarrassed?

74. How many people could you make smile today?

75. What is the hardest thing about school?

76. What is the easiest thing about school?

77. What could we do today to make it great?

78. What is something special we could do for someone else?

79. What can you do today to make yourself a better person?

80. What is the funniest thing you have ever seen?

81. Tell me a funny joke.

82. Do you like to pray?

83. What could we pray for together?

84. What is one thing you would like to learn how to do?

85. What can I do to help you learn that?

86. Do you ever feel nervous?

87. What makes you nervous?

88. Which of your friends like to argue the most?

89. Why do people argue?

90. What kind of things can you do to stop a fight?

91. Do you have any dreams of doing something? What is that dream?

92. Has anyone ever dared you to do something you knew you shouldn't do? Did you do it?

93. What are five things you wish I knew about you?

94. Name five things you are thankful for in your life?

95. What is your most special possession?

96. Would you sell your most special possession if someone offered you money?

97. Are you patient?

98. What can you do to be more patient?

99. Which things or situations can hard for you?

100. If you had three wishes what would you wish for?

101. If you could solve one problem in the world what would it be?

102. Name three of your strengths.

103. Name three of your weaknesses.

104. What do you love most about your sister/brother?

105. What do you dislike most about your sister/brother?

106. What do you like most about me?

107. What do you like least about me?

108. Who would you most like to be like and why?

109. If you could go back in time is there something you would change?

110. Have you ever made a bad choice or a mistake?

111. What is that bad choice or mistake?

112. Have you ever made a good choice?

113. What was that good choice?

114. What do you think of people who do bad things?

115. What do you think of people who do good things?

116. What are you most proud of?

117. What are you least proud of?

118. Why do we give gifts to others?

119. What is the best Christmas present you have ever received?

120. What is your favourite Christmas song?

121. What place do you dream about visiting?

122. Name something you think would be fun to do.

123. What person do you dream about meeting?

124. What adventure do you dream about having?

125. What do you dream about studying?

126. What jobs do you dream about having?

127. Who do you most like to play with?

128. Who do you like to visit the most?

129. How are you like Mommy?

130. How are you like Daddy?

131. How are you like your sister/brother?

132. How are you like your friends?

133. If you had wings where would you fly?

134. If you could be a mermaid/merman would you be?

135. If you could be any animal which one would it be?

136. What's your favourite thing to do with Mommy?

137. What's your favourite thing to do with Daddy?

138. If you could be in any book which book would it be?

139. If you could be in any movie which movie would it be?

140. Tell me one thing that scares you.

141. What could you do when you're scared to make it less scary?

142. Would you rather give up TV, candy or your friends?

143. Who's the worst person in the world?

144. What does heaven look like?

145. What is the most disgusting thing you can think of?

146. If you could change one law what would it be?

147. What's the hardest thing about being a kid?

148. What are three things you have learnt today?

149. What does Dad do for work?

150. What does Mom do for work?

151. If you were going to spend one year on a desert island and could only take three things with you what would they be?

152. Who is your favourite aunt or uncle?

153. Why do you like him or her so much?

154. Name a time that your feelings got hurt.

155. Name a time that you were really mad at me.

156. What's the difference between smart and wise?

157. What's the difference between being happy and kind?

158. What person in history would you like to visit?

159. What sound really annoys you?

160. If you could be any sound what would it be?

161. If you could choose a new name for yourself what would it be and why?

162. What's the coolest thing you have ever seen someone do?

163. What can you do to cheer up others?

164. If you could pick something in your bedroom that would last forever what would it be?

165. If you could spend your time doing only one activity what would it be?

166. If you could shrink any animal in the world and keep it as a pet which animal would you choose?

167. What's your favourite word and why do you like it?

168. What is one thing you think you will be great at when you are an adult and why?

169. If you had to live in the zoo which animal would you be?

170. If you were able to create a new country what would you call it? What would it be like?

171. If you could invite any person in the world to dinner who would it be?

172. If you were a great inventor what would you invent?

173. What is your favourite thing about summer?

174. What is your favourite thing about winter?

175. Where in the world would you most like to live?

176. What do you do when you are feeling really angry?

177. What do you do when you are feeling really sad?

178. What do you think the meaning of life is?

179. When you are an adult how are you going to parent your children differently?

180. What would you do if you saw someone being teased?

181. What would you do if you saw someone being bullied?

182. If you could change one thing about school what would it be?

183. If you could redecorate your room what changes would you make?

184. If you were to receive a present right now what would you want it to be?

185. What is the bravest thing you have ever done?

186. What is more important – money or happiness?

187. What do you wish you had more time for?

188. What makes you unique?

189. Who do you admire and why?

190. Name five people you could go to if you needed help.

191. Why did you pick those people?

192. What would you do if you were invisible for one day?

193. If you could be any type of sandwich what would you be and why?

194. What is your favourite thing to do inside?

195. What is your favourite thing to do outside?

196. What is the best dream you ever had?

197. If we went to the grocery store what would you want me to buy?

198. What is your favourite room in this house?

199. What is your least favourite room in this house?

200. If you could be anywhere right now in this world where would you be and why?

201. What is the silliest face you can make?

202. What is your favourite weather and why?

203. What is your favourite smell and why?

204. What would you do if you won a million dollars?

205. Who is the richest person in the world? How do you know they are rich?

206. If you could only keep one toy which toy would you keep?

207. If you could only keep one book which book would it be?

208. What is your favourite outfit?

209. Have you ever lost something you like? What did you do?

210. Name someone you can trust. Why?

211. What is your favourite ice-cream flavour?

212. What was the best party you have ever been to? What made it so fun?

213. What would you do if you had no TV?

214. How can I tell that you are happy?

215. How can I tell that you are sad?

216. What is the best surprise you have ever had?

217. What is the prettiest thing you have ever seen?

218. What makes you smile?

219. What is your favourite chore to do in the house?

220. What is your least favourite chore to do in the house?

221. If you could play any instrument which would you choose and why?

222. What is your favourite snack?

223. Would you rather: own a boat or plane?

224. Would you rather: be able to fly or be invisible?

225. Would you rather: live in the future or the past?

226. Would you rather: holiday at the beach or the snow?

227. Would you rather: live in the city or the country?

228. Would you rather: live in space or under the sea?

229. Would you rather: eat a bowl full of grasshoppers or worms?

230. Would you rather: meet a vampire or a werewolf?

231. Would you rather: get even or get over it?

232. Would you rather: trust everyone or trust no one?

233. Would you rather: give bad advice or take bad advice?

234. Would you rather: always lose or never play?

235. Would you rather: know it all or have it all?

236. Would you rather: have 10 million dollars or find true love?

237. Would you rather: sing every word you speak or always speak in rhymes?

238. Would you rather: go water-skiing over shark-infested waters or hang-glide over a forest fire?

239. Would you rather: be known for your intelligence or your courage?

240. Would you rather: have all your friends be smarter than you or all your friends be much better looking than you?

241. Would you rather: not wash your hair for a month or not wash your hands for a month?

242. Would you rather: eat ice-cream flavoured poop or poop-flavoured ice-cream?

243. Would you rather: go without TV or junk food for the rest of your life?

244. Would you rather: be a deep sea diver or an astronaut?

245. Would you rather: be able to stop time or fly?

246. Would you rather: visit a dentist or a doctor?

247. Would you rather: only be able to whisper or only be able to shout?

248. Would you rather: eat pizza or cookies?

249. Would you rather: be a firefighter or a policeman?

250. Would you rather: have smelly feet or bad breath?

251. Would you rather: stay up late or get up early?

252. Would you rather: be really tall or really short?

253. Would you rather: be inside all day or outside all day?

254. Would you rather: be able to ONLY eat your favourite food for the rest of your life or never eat your favourite food again?

255. Would you rather: be super-fast or super strong?

256. Would you rather: always have to say what you are thinking or never speak again?

257. Would you rather: never shower again or never brush your teeth again?

258. Would you rather: only eat carrots or only apples for one whole day?

259. Would you rather: live in a place that was always very hot or a place that was always very cold?

260. Would you rather: have breakfast in a hot air balloon or dinner in a castle?

261. Would you rather: live the life of a dog or the life of a cat?

262. Would you rather: read a book or watch a movie?

263. Would you rather: have a dog head with a human body or human head with a dog body?

264. Would you rather: read minds or tell the future?

265. Would you rather: meet an alien or a superhero?

266. Would you rather: have ten brothers or ten sisters?

267. Would you rather: be a famous actor or singer?

268. Would you rather: have the head the size of an orange or watermelon?

269. Would you rather: have a strict teacher who taught you a lot or an easy teacher who taught you not much?

270. Would you rather: be able to control the weather or talk to animals?

271. Would you rather: have green teeth or green hair?

272. Would you rather: have your own private jet or island?

273. Would you rather: be a ninja or a pirate?

274. Would you rather: build a snowman or a sand castle?

275. Would you rather: eat all your food hot or all your food cold?

276. Would you rather: have no electricity or no running water?

277. Would you rather: take the escalator or take the elevator?

278. Would you rather: have a koala or a kangaroo as a pet?

279. Would you rather: have x-ray vision or bionic hearing?

280. Would you rather: have a snake or rat in your room?

281. Would you rather: have a pet dinosaur or a pet alien?

282. Would you rather: be known for being kind or honest?

283. Would you rather: go into the past and meet your ancestors or go into your future and meet your great-great-great-grandchildren?

284. Would you rather be Batman or Spiderman?

285. Would you rather: receive cash or presents?

286. Would you rather: explore space or the ocean?

287. Would you rather: be a kid your whole life or an adult your whole life?

288. Would you rather: end all wars or end world hunger?

289. Would you rather: hear the good news or bad news first?

290. Would you rather: be too busy or too bored?

291. Would you rather: sew all your clothes or grow all your food?

292. Would you rather: have a cook or have a maid?

293. Would you rather: be the youngest or oldest sibling?

294. Would you rather: be a little late or really early?

295. Would you rather: have your first child at 18 or 40?

296. Would you rather: be stuck on a train or a bus?

297. Would you rather: change your eye colour or your hair colour?

298. Would you rather: write a famous book or a famous song?

299. Would you rather be fluent in another language or master every musical instrument?

300. Would you rather: be an Olympic Gold medallist or an Academy Award winner?

Once again I want to stress the importance of speaking to your children. As Abigail Van Buren noted if you want your children to turn out well spend twice as much time with them and half as much money. In case I need to spell it out for you in further detail this means spending TIME with children is more important than spending MONEY on children.

When your children are talking to you about their concerns STOP whatever you are doing and LISTEN to them. Express interest in what they are saying, however trivial it may seem at the time. And let them finish before you respond – don't be a one-upper who always jumps straight in with how the story relates back to you.

If your child knows you are willing to listen then they will continue coming to you with their thoughts and problems. So do your best to maintain that open line of communication and allow them the opportunity to feel heard. You can do this by talking to your children like they are human beings who have a voice and deserve to share it.

Children are great imitators so give them something great to imitate. Start by making the time today and eventually talking together will become a natural, regular and favorite part of your day.

TIP 56: KEEP YOUR CHILD SAFE

Better to be safe than sorry. American Proverb.

As soon as there is life there is danger. Ralph Waldo Emerson.

We all want to keep our kids safe and secure and preventing injuries and harm from befalling children with special needs is not so different from those without disabilities.

To keep your child safe you will need to:

- Know and consider what things are unique concerns or a danger for your child

- Plan ways to protect your child from harm and injury and share the plan with others.

- Remember your child's needs will change over time so be prepared to adapt your plan.

I won't pretend to know your situation but I will make an educated guess and assume your child's safety is of upmost importance to you. It is for me especially as my son has - in addition to his disability - the added bonus of quite a few serious allergies. So I need to always be super cautious about food – not only about preparing meals and snacks that are egg-, dairy- and nut-free but making sure he is in a safe environment without the risk of exposure to these allergens. For my son carelessness about food could potentially lead to death so you may appreciate how fanatical I am about safety in this area.

This is however not the only area of safety that parents need to consider. You may have a child with limited ability to move, see, hear, or make decisions, or perhaps your son or daughter does not feel or understand pain and might not realize that something is unsafe or might have trouble getting away.

Whichever category your child falls into please know we all share this responsibility in making sure that our children stay physically and mentally safe. This responsibility also falls onto the school, the community and the government, so if you feel your child's safety is being compromised please speak up immediately.

HOW TO PREPARE YOUR KIDS FOR SAFETY IN THE OUTSIDE WORLD

- Teach your child to never, ever to get into a car or walk off with a stranger.

- Make sure your child understands that in your family no-one ever keeps secrets. Children should never allow ANYONE to swear them to secrecy. This includes people they think they can trust.

- Teach your child to swim. If children are not entirely confident then they must be supervised at all times near water.

- Teach your child road-safety and how to cross the road properly. I was taught: *look left, look right then left again. Are there any cars? Fine now we can cross."*

- Teach your child to recognise danger – WHO can they trust (and who they can't), WHAT is appropriate behavior (and what isn't) and WHERE it is safe (and where it isn't safe to be).

- Teach your child that while most people are fine there are some bad folk in this world who could hurt him or her. They should understand it's important to stay safe and trust their instincts. They should never do anything they don't feel comfortable doing.

- Teach your child it's okay to ask for help.

HOW TO KEEP YOUR KIDS SAFE IN THE DIGITAL WORLD

We have come to a time in history where most children, even those with special needs, are capable of using an iPad or computer. Some are even encouraged to use these devices as an educational or communication tool. Consequently children today spend way more time utilizing these gadgets than we ever did as kids on our Gameboys and Atari systems. (Who am I kidding? My parents didn't ever buy me any electronic device so I had zero experience playing video games as a kid).

There's a big difference now though between those early gaming systems and what our kids have now. It's called the Internet. As fantastic as the Internet is it is way too easy for children today to stray into the dangerous side of things because the digital world is very different from the real world in which we live.

Here are some basic rules to help keep your children safe on the Internet:

- Keep your child's computer or iPad centrally located so that you can keep an eye on what your child is viewing or doing.

- Teach your kids to never, ever give out personal information like name, age, address, school names, photos or passwords.

- Use common-sense precautions like firewalls, virus protection and parental controls. This is an absolute must. To not do so is like leaving the front door to your house open all night.

- Understand the high risk of internet bullying or trolling. Statistics vary but at least 20% of children will receive hateful, harassing or insulting messages over the computer. If your child is being harassed they should either tell you about it or refrain from using the website.

- Make sure your child understands they are NEVER to meet any online friend alone. If they are old enough to chat online (not appropriate for my children yet – this is something I am hoping they will avoid) then they should also use a nickname that will not reveal who they really are.

- Finally feel free to set some limits. If you feel like your child is spending way too much time on his computer or device set some new ground rules that you feel more comfortable with. Once the rules are set be consistent and make sure they are followed.

TIP 57: DON'T CLIP YOUR CHILD'S WINGS

There are two gifts we should give our children.
One is roots; the other is wings.

You are probably wondering what I mean when I say *don't clip your child's wings*. This term is often used in relation to bird owners who are advised to clip the wings of their birds for their own safety. Clipping a bird's wings is done so it can help limit the animal's access to dangers such as windows and ceiling fans and it also ensures your pet does not accidentally fly away. This consequently forces the bird to be dependent on its owner which many people believe strengthens the bond between humans and animal.

Others believe however that depriving a bird of its ability to fly causes physical and psychological damage. Clipped birds tend to be more passive and compliant than unclipped birds because they are unable to make independent choices about where they can go and when. They are basically a captive to their perch.

So how does this relate to parenting a special needs child? I just want you to be mindful of the fact you may be clipping your child's wings without even realising it. Even kids with special needs have a desire to soar through the sky of life – they like to be daring and constantly push limits and they also like to rise to the challenge of accomplishing more than everyone else imagines they can. A lot of us however find it difficult to watch our children make mistakes and consequently feel like they would be safer if they were stuck sitting on their safe perch.

Firstly I want you to know it isn't only your special needs child who is prone to making mistakes (again and again). Rest assured your child is not alone. Everyone makes mistakes – both those who are able-bodied and those who aren't. Secondly I want you to understand how important it is to try and feel joyful and embrace your child's desire to fly. If he or she is blessed with tenacity and courage then that is something to be treasured and nurtured rather than something you need to feel stifled or frightened about.

Clipping your wings is a phrase that is synonymous with holding a person back. It means: to restrain someone, to reduce or put an end to his or her privileges, to restrict someone's freedom or thwart his or her ambition. Now I am pretty confident that we don't intentionally mean to clip our children's wings but I want you to ask yourself this now: is there any way in which you may be inadvertently limiting your child? Do you suggest not trying something simply because you are worried your child might fail instead of encouraging him or her to give it a go and enjoy the experience? Do you obsess about all the things that can go wrong instead of focusing on the things that could go right?

Try to change your view about your child's desire to dream big and soar high, instead of constantly worrying about him or her landing with a thud and possibly breaking a bone or two along the way. Sure there will be a few thuds, maybe lots of them along the way and even a broken bone or two but the joy and satisfaction that comes from trying, from knowing that you lived a life without regrets, will far outweigh those stumbles. After all in the end we only regret the chances we didn't take. It is far better to do something and regret it than regret not doing it at all. Because there are no regrets in life, just lessons learned.

TIP 58: EXPLAIN TO YOUR CHILD WHY YOUR VALUES ARE IMPORTANT

Values are like fingerprints. Nobody's are the same but you leave them all over everything you do. Elvis Presley.

It's not hard to make decisions once you know what your values are. Roy E. Disney.

I think one of the most important things we can do is explain to our children what are values are because it truly underlies all our behavior. When I was young my parents thought the two most important values were honesty and respect. Because there were so clear and consistent with their belief about their importance I understood automatically why I was getting in trouble if I ever spoke in an abrupt or rude manner (one word: disrespectful) or arrived to a function late (again, disrespectful). They also expected and rewarded honesty; dishonesty – not so much, which is why to this day I still dislike it when people like to fudge the truth. Growing up these two values – respect and honesty - became so ingrained in me they now feel like they are a part of my DNA because my parents never swerved from or altered their opinion of their importance.

Now I am raising my own children I find that in addition to valuing respect and honesty I have own set of values that I think are important. Like independence, harmony and freedom of choice (values that were not necessarily important to my parents). We all uphold certain values that dictate our preferred lifestyle, career and family life and when we're clear about our values, we make our decisions consistently, proactively and with confidence.

Take a look now at some of the possible values that a person may hold and note the ones that stand out to you as being important.

- Abundance
- Acceptance
- Advancement
- Adventure
- Ambition
- Animal Rights
- Art
- Authenticity
- Authority
- Balance
- Beauty
- Calmness
- Challenge
- Change
- Charity
- Collaboration
- Community
- Compassion
- Competence
- Competition
- Courage
- Creativity
- Cultural
- diversity
- Curiosity
- Decisiveness
- Democracy
- Discipline
- Empathy
- Environment
- Equality
- Excitement
- Experimentation
- Expertise
- Fairness
- Family
- Fashion
- Feminism
- Financial Security
- Flexibility
- Forgiveness
- Frankness
- Freedom of choice
- Freedom with time
- Time
- Friendships
- Fun

- Generosity
- Global
- Awareness
- Happiness
- Harmony
- Having a voice
- Health
- Helping Others
- Helping
- Society
- Honesty
- Honour
- Human Rights
- Humor
- Imagination
- Independence
- Influence
- Innovation
- Inspiration
- Integrity
- Intellectual status
- Intelligence
- Kindness
- Knowledge
- Laughter
- Leadership
- Learning
- Leisure
- Literature
- Living my
- dreams
- Love
- Making a
- difference
- Making
- decisions
- Music
- Nature
- Open communication
- Optimism
- Organization
- Passion
- Patriotism
- Peace
- Persistence
- Personal expression
- Personal growth

- Physical challenge
- Play
- Pleasure
- Positive
- attitude
- Power
- Professionalism
- Quality of Life
- Recognition
- Reflection
- Relationships
- Relaxation
- Reliability
- Respect
- Responsibility
- Results
- Risk taking
- Security
- Self-Love
- Self-Respect
- Sensuality
- Spirituality
- Spontaneity
- Stability
- Style
- Support
- Taking care of myself
- Taking risks
- The big picture
- Tolerance
- Tranquillity
- Trust
- Understanding
- Variety
- Wealth
- Wonder

It's quite a list isn't it? If you are anything like me then quite a few values probably struck a chord with you. If you haven't worked out what your true values are as yet I think it would be valuable for you to do so. Sit down right now and try to narrow down your list to your five to eight core values.

Why? Because your values dictate much of your behavior and disciplining strategies at home. If you are conscious about which particular values are of importance to you and you communicate this to your family you breed understanding and you will feel more confident being consistent in your approach.

Remember this: the decisions you make are a result of your values and these are reflected in your life in many ways. At the end of the day it's your essence and your values that are most important. These will be easier to pass onto your children when they know why they are so important and when they see and learn these lessons through your actions every day.

TIP 59: HAVE A GRATITUDE JOURNAL

Gratitude can transform common days into thanksgivings, turn routine jobs into joy, and change ordinary opportunities into blessings. William Arthur Ward.

Showing gratitude is one of simplest yet most powerful things humans can do for each other. Randy Pausch.

I know I have said it before but I will say it again: there is always something to be thankful for. Yes even if you live a life that is fraught with difficulties, even if you have a child with special needs, there is something beautiful within each of your days. Whether it's a smile you didn't expect to receive, the sight of a breathtakingly wonderful sunrise or the support of a friend who was there exactly when you needed them most these are all gifts to be treasured and ones which you can feel grateful for.

Being grateful turns what we have into enough and we can choose to be grateful no matter what. Some people tend to think happiness comes as a result of getting something we don't have when in actual fact it's the other way around – happiness is instead the recognizing and appreciating of what we already have. Because it's not happy people who are thankful, it's the thankful people who are happy.

So what are you grateful for today? I recommend purchasing a journal – it can be as simple or pretty as you like – and writing down five things every day you are grateful for. Don't think you can come up with five things every day? Well give it a go, you might surprise yourself. Even though I have just experienced a crazy week with at least one child home sick from school every day (plus I myself am on the verge of coming down with a chest infection too) I can still think of many things for which I am grateful.

For example, today I am grateful for:

- Medicine
- A comfortable bed in which I can rest
- Herbal teas
- Warm baths
- Hugs and kisses from my kids
- The unwavering devotion from my dog
- The gift of life

Appreciate everything you have RIGHT NOW because a lot of people often take for granted the things that most deserve our gratitude but don't realize it until they are gone. And you don't want that realization to come too late. You want to appreciate it now, while it is still there to be thankful for.

The more you express gratitude for what you have, the more you will find to express gratitude for. If that isn't enough to convince you to start keeping a gratitude journal consider this: studies have found there are numerous impressive benefits to writing down things for which we are grateful. These benefits include better sleep, less illness and significantly more happiness in individuals who choose to focus their attention on all the positive things in their life. If you like you can also consider starting a journal as a family so your child enjoys the benefits too.

TIP 60: STOP LETTING FEAR

RULE YOUR LIFE

Everything you want is on the other side of fear. Jack Canfield.

The only thing we have to fear is fear itself. Franklin D. Roosevelt.

Fear defeats more people than any other thing in the world. Ralph Waldo Emerson.

One of my favorite books is called Fear the Fear and Do It Anyway by Susan Jeffers. I think it perfectly sums up everything we feel and think about fear and how to go about rectifying it. Fear is without a doubt a very real emotion induced by a perceived threat in the outside world. Fear usually occurs in response to a specific stimulus occurring in the present or to a future situation which we perceive to be a risk to our health, life, security, status or anything else we deem to be valuable.

The first thing we need to accept as parents of special needs kids is that feeling fear is normal. We feel scared as a result of so many reasons – we fear our children will be hurt, we fear they will not be accepted or loved, we fear they will be unhappy or let down by life. All of these fears seem valid to us because deep down we know there is a chance those things may come to fruition. There's a chance our kids may be unaccepted, depressed, confused, or unloved.

I can tell you one thing though, feeling fear about these situations doesn't make the situation go away. To the contrary it may end up backfiring on you or even being counter-productive and in the end the thing you feared the most comes to light purely because that was what you chose to spend most of your time and energy focusing on.

Nothing stands in the way of progress and change more than fear. Fear is the ultimate mind-killer. Fear is like a prison that keeps you locked in a state of inaction and indecision. The only way to get over your fears is to accept they exist and move on from it. Refuse to give fear the power to control your life because if you can overcome your fears, and take action in spite of feeling scared, you can move forward to becoming stronger and wiser within yourself.

Decide today that what you want – maybe its desire for your child to be happy and included – is more important than feeling scared about it not happening. Let your faith be bigger than your fear because thinking and procrastinating will not help you overcome your fears but ACTIONS will. Like Susan Jeffers so wisely said: feel the fear and do it anyway. Allow love guide you in your actions and let your actions be guided by confidence rather than fear. For that is the key to change – simply let go of your fear. After all the only way around it is through it.

TIP 61: TRUST YOUR INSTINCTS

You have permission to walk away from anything that doesn't feel right. Trust your instincts and listen to your inner-voice – it's trying to protect you. Bryant McGill.

When it comes to kids I believe a parent usually knows their child best. You have raised your baby since his first breath, you know his quirks, his likes and dislikes and even without him saying a word (or even when he says a word that would have you believe otherwise) you instinctively know when something is wrong.

During our journey as parents of special needs kids there will be numerous times when we will be guided by the experience of doctors and teachers. Their knowledge will be requested, examined, mulled over and ultimately much appreciated and valued. Then there will be other times when their guidance doesn't sit quite right with us. Maybe they offered a diagnosis that doesn't make sense or they offered a solution to a problem that you know deep down will only make things worse.

My advice to you if you ever get that little voice in your head, funny tingle in your tummy or bad feeling that just doesn't go away is this: STOP AND LISTEN. As humans we are born with certain instincts to help us survive and I believe our gut instinct is one of them. You may also recognize this as something called your intuition, which is simply when you "know" something without being able to explain how or why you came to the conclusion rationally.

If you are like me you will probably question or second guess your intuition sometimes. It can feel strange to go against the grain or base important decisions on something you don't truly understand. If that's the case I want you to understand your intuition actually taps into your subconscious mind where you archive all sorts of information that you can't recall on a more conscious level. We are honestly so much more intelligent and attuned to the world than we often give ourselves credit for. Even if our feelings seem to defy logic they can often still be warranted.

This is why I think it's so important you trust your first gut instinct. If you feel deep down in your heart and soul that something is wrong it probably is. Don't hesitate to ask questions if you feel the wrong treatment is being offered. It's fine to stop and ask more questions – your child will appreciate your care and questioning. After all your heart knows things that your mind can't explain.

TIP 62: MANAGE YOUR FRUSTRAIONS

Frustration, although quite painful at times, is a very positive and essential part of success. Bo Bennett.

Expectation is the mother of all frustration. Antonio Banderas.

So what is frustration? I'm pretty sure we have all felt this emotion at one stage – I myself experience it on a daily basis (lucky me!). For the record frustration is defined as that awful feeling of disappointment or dissatisfaction, often fueled by anger and annoyance, when a person is stopped from reaching a desired goal. It's a feeling that comes from expecting others to act or react in a way that you want that them to (and of course they don't).

The truth is when we achieve our goals we feel happy. Actually it's more than happiness - we feel great, satisfied and content. We feel like celebrating! But when we don't achieve our goals - well we then say hello to the opposite emotions of irritability, annoyance, anger and emotional fatigue. We feel like things just aren't sitting right with the world and we desperately want the situation to be rectified, preferably RIGHT NOW.

Unfortunately in life things aren't always going to go our way. No amount of crying, screaming, pouting or fuming is ever going to change that. Kids will fight, keys will be misplaced, cars will break down, and buses will be missed. Life will always be filled with one pothole of frustration after another. There will be minor irritations which get resolved within a few minutes all the way to the major issues of continued failure of a desired goal. Of course those ones seriously suck and when I say suck I mean they suck away at all your patience, inner peace and energy.

So what should we do when we are feeling frustrated? Firstly I think we need to understand all frustrations are ultimately self-induced. Sure the outside world can invite us to become upset, worried or scared but it's up to us to accept the invitation and act out on it.

My biggest frustration comes from expecting my two children to be the greatest of friends. Fine so I'm probably setting myself up for disappointment with a goal like this. But it would be nice if they could pass through one full day without torturing their sibling with a smartass comment or getting involved in a silly fight.

When I hear my kids squabble, even if it's just for five minutes out of the whole day it makes me feel both frustrated and annoyed. I want their squabbling to stop and when it doesn't it puts me in a sour mood. Admittedly I have trained myself to snap out of this mood fairly quickly but still I can feel my blood beginning to boil every time I hear a child call "Mommmmm, so-and-so is annoying me!"

In case you haven't guessed the obvious solution to my frustration I will clue you in. First it has to do with having realistic expectations. I have already set myself up for disappointment by expecting my children to be best buddies who never have a fight. Was I myself best friends with my sisters when I was young? No way.

Sure we are closer now that we are older, wiser and no longer live in each other's pockets but back when I was still living at home I considered both my little sisters to be annoying pests. I hated it when they wouldn't respect my personal space or continually got me into trouble for doing nothing wrong (for the record: when you are young everyone else is the culprit.) Is this normal? Yes. And do other families have kids who fight? You betcha.

If I stopped right now and decided to accept that siblings are always going to fight then that thought alone would reduce my frustration levels by a great percentage. If I accepted that hospital appointments would often be booked at a time that wasn't convenient to me (forcing me to change my work day), if I accepted that sometimes my child's disability would negatively impact where we could go (and we would have to miss out) and that life was going to regularly throw me lemons (and those lemons would only make crappy, indigestible lemonade) then hey, maybe that would eliminate the rest of my frustration too.

Because that is what causes most of our frustration: unrealistic expectations and expecting things and people to always behave or work perfectly. News alert: there is no such thing as perfection. Of course it's normal to feel frustrated every now and then when things don't go your way but if you feel like you are constantly losing it over trivial things consider the following tips:

1. Take a deep breath – count to ten or even a hundred, however long you need, until you calm down.
2. Talk to a friend – find a neutral party who you can vent to during times of need.
3. Accept reality – if things aren't working out maybe it's time to change your attitude or behavior instead.
4. Take a walk – it will help clear your mind.
5. If you can't step out of the house do something else that is healthy and productive.
6. Stop blaming yourself – it isn't always your fault. Or if you do feel partly to blame consider finding another way to approach the problem.
7. Remember this too shall pass – it always does.

TIP 63: HELP YOUR CHILD MANAGE HIS OR HER OWN FRUSTRATIONS

I know this may sound like a repetitive tip but it isn't. That's because the frustrations parents experience on a daily basis – the car won't start, bank funds are low, work is stressful or the kids are having yet ANOTHER fight – pale in comparison to the type of frustrations that a child with special needs is forced to face every day.

I will use my own son as an example. He has a physical disability which impacts both his gross motor and fine motor skills. This means he finds tasks other kids deem simple – like doing up buttons, zippers, opening and closing containers, putting on shoes and socks – either difficult or near impossible. Even though he knows and understands this comes along with the territory of having Charcot Marie Tooth disease that doesn't stop him from feeling frustrated every time he tries to be more independent yet hits a brick wall with his attempts.

One of the greatest tools we can give our children with special needs is the tool of managing their frustration. Why? This is because most of their frustration comes from an internal rather than external source. From the moment our children wake up they are barraged with more hurdles than most able-bodied and able-minded person may have to face in a year.

When I was a young sleep-deprived mom I fell down a flight of stairs (after skipping a step) which resulted in one broken foot and severely torn ligaments in the other. This left me immobile for three months and the best I could do was crawl around the house while tending to an eight month old baby and energetic two-year-old toddler. Everything was a challenge to me then – cleaning the house, cooking meals and going out to run errands (I depended on the shopping center's mobility scooters which were kindly brought to my car and collected from my parking spot at the end of my shopping expeditions.)

I realized at that point for the first time in my life how blessed I was previously to have two working feet that enabled me to walk through life, fulfilling all my goals without a second thought. Now I know and understand full well the challenges my son faces on a daily basis and how much frustration he faces as a result of his mobility issues. I have walked in those same shoes for just three months and they were some of the hardest days in my life.

So what can you do to help your child who may also require help to do simple, everyday tasks? Thankfully there is a lot you can help them manage their daily frustrations. Some tips include:

1. GIVING THEM A HELPING HAND

Let your child know she is not alone and that there will always be something to help her with the things she finds difficult. At eight, I do not expect my son to do anything he is not physically capable of doing. I am happy to help him get dressed, put on his shoes and socks and pack and carry his heavy school bag to his classroom. Once he is at school he has the fortune of having a teacher's aide who is there to assist him with tasks he finds difficult. He does not have to ever worry or stress about trying to master things that are beyond his abilities. And because he is free from this pressure he can focus instead on all the things he IS capable of doing.

2. TEACH YOUR CHILD COPING TOOLS AND STRATEGIES

I mentioned in the previous tip things you can do when you are feeling stressed and frustrated and the same strategies can be applied by your child. Teach your child to learn to breathe deeply when he is feeling overwhelmed, to learn to count to a ten before over-reacting, to speak about the feelings he is having, to focus instead on the things he CAN do, and to have a positive attitude in times of stress and frustration.

3. LET YOUR CHILD KNOW THE NATURE OF THEIR DISABILITY AND WHAT IS TO BE EXPECTED

It helps a child greatly to know the things he or she is experiencing are a direct result of their disability or diagnosis and not because they are weird/stupid/silly/crazy/not trying hard enough. My son has always understood there are three common characteristics to Charcot Marie Tooth Disease. Firstly people with this diagnosis struggle with stairs, secondly they have poor balance, and thirdly they fatigue quickly. So whenever he has participated in a physical education where the kids have been asked to hop he has always known this is something he isn't able to do and he has spoken up about it. "Sorry but I can't hop because I have CMT."

Whenever he gets tired he knows it isn't because he is lazy but because it is normal for a CMT kid. Finally because his hands are now impacted too (another natural progression for kids with CMT) he knows to speak up if he is struggling with buttons, zippers, lids, or if his hands are getting tired when writing. In the instance of disabilities, knowledge is without a doubt power.

4. FOCUS ON WHAT YOUR CHILD IS GOOD AT

Even if your child struggles with tasks that other children find easy there will definitely be something else they are good at. Find out what that is and focus on their skill in this arena instead. In the case of my son he may be physically challenged but mentally he is super smart. He is incredibly gifted when it comes to academics and finds school work easy to complete. I am grateful for this because I am certain it will help him in the future when it comes to going to college and choosing a career. He has always excelled in reading, science and mathematics, which is a source of much pride for him.

Maybe your child isn't great at the same things but he or she will have their own special thing you would benefit from nurturing. Are they good at art, drawing, writing, speaking, gaming, sport, building things or being helpful and kind? Do they think outside the square? Do they have their own unique way of doing things? Whatever it is they are good at NURTURE it and encourage your child to pursue this passion. Knowing they are good at something will help reduce their frustration in other areas of their life.

TIP 64: PROVIDE INFORMATION TO YOUR CHILD'S CLASS

When my son first started school we found it wasn't necessary to give a detailed explanation about his condition to his classmates. Even though they were in kindergarten his peers intuitively understood his feet worked slower than everyone else's. Without any adult encouragement they bestowed my son with more caring and support than he probably needed (but hey, he didn't mind. There is seriously nothing better than feeling loved and accepted by everyone!)

As he got older though the care and support from his friends still continued but now there was also confusion. They were beginning to ask questions: but WHY does he walk slower? WHY does he find some easy things hard? Why? Why? Why? In grade two I spoke with my son about the idea of someone coming to his classroom to explain exactly what Charcot Marie Tooth Disease is (or CMT as he calls it) to his peers but initially he hesitated. He didn't like the idea of everyone making a big deal about his condition (he said it would be embarrassing!) but by grade three the potential embarrassment was far outweighed by the possibility of his classmates becoming more knowledgeable about his condition.

I enlisted the help of his fabulous occupational therapist and also my eldest daughter who had recently completed a big project on the human nervous system (she had decided to focus on CMT so she too could learn more about the condition). Their combined presentation to the class included lots of models (demonstrating the way a "good" nerve worked versus a "faulty" nerve for example) and experiments.

The children had to wear thick garden gloves while trying to do lots of different activities which depended on good fine-motor skills. They had to also wear heavily weighted shoes and try to do simple things like hop with them on. Not surprisingly the kids struggled a lot with limited function of both their feet and hands. So for the first time ever they really understood what it was like for my son to function with his CMT and they felt that through experience.

Now I am not assuming your own child's disability or condition will be something that can be demonstrated in the same way that my son's was. But perhaps it can be. Maybe there are interesting videos or presentations that accurately convey the way your child feels physically, emotionally or socially. Maybe there are books on the topic. Maybe there is even someone older and wiser with the same condition that would be happy to come in and speak with your child's classmates. Whatever method works for you consider taking the opportunity to educate your school or friends about your child's condition because the more we educate others the more we spread awareness and awareness will help breed acceptance.

TIP 65: KEEP YOUR RECORDS IN A SAFE PLACE

If you are anything like me then over the years you have acquired a stack of paperwork all to do with your child's condition and its subsequent treatment. At first I filed away these reports with all my other important papers like house insurance forms and car registration slips until I realized how often I needed to refer to them. Now I store them in colored folders specifically marked with my child's name and I've accumulated so much paperwork these folders are now stored in their own box. I have also separated them according to their category – medical and hospital reports, physiotherapy and occupational therapy, school forms, insurance papers, mobility aid information and requests, associations and things to investigate etcetera.

It is essential you keep all your important papers and reports in a safe place because they probably include information that will be pertinent to others, even if they are no longer so important to you. Don't stress - it doesn't matter if you haven't been organized your papers before today. Just go back and do your best to find everything that has to do with your child and store it in a folder. You can properly organize it another day in a way that works best for you.

Do the same with your email account – start a new folder labelled with your child's name and move across any emails you have received in the past about his treatment or medical condition. You may wish to print these emails out too so you have a backup copy for your records. Being organized about your records will make you feel more focused and less stressed (about not being organized!)

TIP 66: HAVE ONE MEAL TOGETHER AS A FAMILY EVERY DAY

Growing up I learned life's most important lessons at the dinner table
- Chef John Besh.

It's been said nothing brings people together like good food. Families that eat together apparently stay together and even if this sounds like far-fetched notion I want you to consider making mealtimes a special time in your family. I know it's unrealistic for us to expect to have all three meals together every day – we all have busy lives and things like work, school and life tends to get in the way of that grand idea. But most of us can pull off at least one meal-time together if we try.

I grew up in a European family where meal times were really important. Even today when I visit my parents the expectation is still that we will sit together as a family, enjoy the food (by not pigging out on something else fifteen minutes before) and have a conversation where we fill each other up on all the latest adventures in our life (however boring). As a kid that was probably the only time my parents really had a chance to focus on me and find out what was going on at school and with my friends because the rest of the time they were simply too busy (busy back then meant working a few jobs and *not* wasting time watching TV or surfing the internet or Facebook).

Meal times were also the only chance I had to speak to my parents and have their undivided attention, because whenever I tried to catch them at different times of the day my dad was usually at work and my mom was either working herself or too busy cooking, cleaning, ironing, washing dishes etcetera.

I'm not saying you don't have time to listen to your children at different times of the day – as parents we are now a lot wiser and worldlier about raising kids than the generation before us was. Back when I was young children were to be seen but not heard which is probably why I considered meal times to be so special, because whilst having dinner those rules did not apply. Even if you do listen to your kids at other times I am sure there is a good chance you have something else on your mind at the same time. Maybe you are trying to work or clean, do your finances or go to the bathroom (we have all been there; kids are like magnets to a parent sitting on a toilet!).

Meal times are that one time of the day where we consciously plan to sit down and relax. So take advantage of this fact. Sit down and enjoy your family's company while you have the opportunity to do so. Family time should be considered sacred time and both respected and protected. Ideally it would be nice if it was at the end of the day, once everyone is home from work and activities, so you can unwind together and talk about how your day was but that isn't always possible (and I know this firsthand as my husband is a shift-worker). If both partners can't make it that's okay – just enjoy the meal with your children.

Talk and ask your children questions. Get them to ask YOU questions. Let them know that it's okay to discuss anything that is on their mind. I myself discovered lots of interesting things about my parents during dinners (like new stories from their childhood) so consider opening up to your children in a similar way. Share with them your life stories and memories, your dreams and knowledge. Make your meal-times special by making them count.

TIP 67: MAKE AN EMERGENCY SHEET

An emergency sheet is a must-have in any family but even more so important when you have a child with special needs. At its most basic level an emergency sheet would include the following information:

- Name
- Address
- Home Phone Number
- Father's Cell Phone Number
- Mother's Cell Phone Number
- Emergency Number (For Fire, Ambulance & Police)
- Hospital (Paediatric Care Unit)
- Poison Control
- Next of Kin Contact

However when it comes to parenting a special needs child a more detailed emergency sheet will no doubt be required. Consider the following details as essential information to include:

- Child's Full Name
- Child's Date of Birth
- Child's Weight (and as of date)
- Child's Medical Conditions
- Child's Allergies
- Child's Specialist
- Current Medications Taken
- Other Special Considerations

There are numerous free templates available on the web so if you would like to have something that looks a bit fancier than a stock standard excel worksheet just google "Emergency Sheet" and choose a template that appeals to you. I recommend you fill in and print out at least four copies – one for your personal records, one for the fridge, one for your handbag or car and another that can travel with your child if he or she is ever visiting family or a friend. You can also make extras for your desk at work, the nanny or babysitter or family members that would prefer to have their own personal copy. Remember to laminate the emergency sheet if you would like to keep it looking good for some time and remember to update the information regularly. After all it's always better to be safe than sorry.

TIP 68: NEVER FORGET WHO YOU ARE

This tip is going to be short and sweet yet to the point.

I want you to never forget who you are. You are a person with hopes, dreams and passions. Only you can satisfy your needs and you alone are enough. Never lose sight of your humanity and how fragile and beautiful this world is. You are precious. Life is precious. You were once a young child with your whole life stretched before you. But time moves quickly and we can never go back. So remember to grasp each moment fully and live in it, abundantly, ever so gratefully...

Even though you are one of seven billion individuals living in this world you are unique, one of a kind and special. It takes forever to find yourself but only one second to forget who you are. So hold onto who you are deep inside – worthy of love, worthy of happiness. Try to enjoy this delicate world, your dear family and your one shot at life while it is all still here to be enjoyed.

TIP 69: CELEBRATE DIFFERENCES

It is not our differences that divide us. It is our inability to recognize, accept and celebrate those differences. Audre Lorde.

They laugh at me because I am different. I laugh at them because they're all the same. Kurt Cobain.

The things that make me different are the things that make me ME. Winnie the Pooh.

One of my favorite songs by Lady Gaga is *Born This Way* purely because it speaks about unconditional acceptance and celebrating differences in people instead of condemning others for being different. As Miss Gaga so eloquently put it in the song it doesn't matter if you are gay, straight or bi, black, white or beige, broke or evergreen – if life's disabilities have left you outcast, bullied or teased then just stop and love yourself today because we were born this way.

I love this idea: that God made us all perfect, that we don't need to change who we inherently are for anybody else because there is nothing there *to be changed*. We were born and made just perfect. I think this is an important point to communicate to our children – that they are indeed perfect just as they are. They need to know that it's okay to be different, that there's nothing with standing out from the crowd or looking, acting or thinking in a way others think is strange or "weird".

Since when was being weird such a bad thing anyway? As an adult I love unique individuals with a story to tell. To me being weird is a compliment, something cool, something that sets you apart from the crowd and makes you feel special. I always tell my kids *"don't be afraid of being different; be afraid of being the same as everyone else."* To confirm this belief I recently bought home a gift for my children – a beautiful plaque which states *"Don't be afraid to be yourself, everyone else is taken."*

There is definitely power in not caring what other people think. There is freedom in feeling brave enough to act silly or to stand apart from the crowd. Every day that you choose to celebrate the differences in your child you teach them to celebrate their uniqueness too. Through example you teach them there is nothing to be ashamed of and everything to be proud of.

TIP 70: DON'T HIDE YOUR CHILD AWAY

I know you would never intentionally set out to isolate your child but sometimes things are just easier when you stay close to home base. I know this first hand even though I myself do try my best to get my children out as often as possible. There are days when I am full of energy and feel invincible – can I pull off an all day trip to the city via a ferry? Sure I can. How about a trip to the zoo where the crowds give new meaning to the term claustrophobia? Absolutely – I'll take it as a challenge. What about a few hours at a fun fair? Well there's no harm in giving it a go.

Then there are days when the idea of packing the ramp and trying to find a parking spot that allows me to unload and upload the power wheelchair is simply over-whelming. I don't have the patience, strength or heart to deal with the crowds or another disappointed look when my child is faced with the cold hard reality of his disability because the world does not always cater to those with limited mobility.

Sometimes our home feels safer and more secure. This is definitely my child's happy place and we love having friends and family over. But I want you to know that just because your home is a safe base that doesn't mean you can't explore the outside world too. Don't hide your child away from the world or life because it's "easier." Be brave enough to set out and explore the world. Yes you will be faced with challenges other parents won't ever have to deal with but that's okay. Just do your best.

Try little excursions first before tackling the big outings. Go out once a month before you think about making it a weekly expedition. Find out what interests your child then consider doing whatever you can to get him or her there – enlist the help of friends, workers, the community or anyone with the power to make it smoothly happen without adding additional stress or worry to your life. Take little steps at first and over time you will build the confidence to take more regular outings and enjoy more of what the world has to offer.

TIP 71: HAVE THE COURAGE TO LET GO

Some people believe holding on and hanging in there are signs of great strength. However there are times when it takes more strength to know when to let go and then do it.

Ann Landers.

Life is really a balance of holding on and letting go. I'm sure we have all read the infamous "Welcome to Holland" essay written by Emily Perl Kingsley in 1987 which uses the metaphor of a travel trip to explain the feelings some parents experience when they discover they have a child with special needs. In the essay it talks about the excitement new parents feel about their impending vacation to Italy, only to discover with much disappointment their plane has landed in Holland.

If you haven't ever come across this essay I urge you to search for it on the Internet right now. I'm sure parts of the essay will resonate with you because as parents of special needs kids we are all similar in that we found ourselves in a destination that we didn't ever intend to visit. But Emily is right is saying even though Holland may not be as flashy or fast-paced as Italy it is still a beautiful place to be. In Holland there are windmills and tulips and it is lovely in a completely different way. I especially love the line which says *"if you spend your life mourning the fact that you didn't get to Italy, you may never be free to enjoy the very special, the very lovely things about Holland."*

To enjoy your life in "Holland" you may find it necessary to let things go of some old dreams; simply for the reason they are either unachievable or too heavy. But please do not be saddened by this act of letting go. To the contrary there is a strange sense of peace that comes from having the courage to let go of what you can't change. And sometimes what you are most afraid of doing is the very thing that will set you free.

As Hermann Hesse so eloquently stated "some of us think that holding on makes us strong; but sometimes it is letting go." So close your eyes. Clear your heart and let the things that are holding you down or keeping you back simply go.

TIP 72: THINK ABOUT YOUR CHILD'S FUTURE

If you have a child who may not be able to make informed decisions about major issues in their life at the age of 18 then it is possible you may need to learn more about guardianship or conservatorship.

A guardian is someone who has the authority to make lifestyle or personal decisions on behalf of a person who is incapable of making these decisions for him or herself. Evidence will usually need to be provided that this person has a decision-making disability or has a disability that results in the person being partially or wholly incapable of managing themselves. A guardian thereafter tends to be responsible for lifestyle or personal decisions such as decisions about medical or dental treatment, living accommodations, finances and what services they need.

Every country is different so please do your research and look into guardianship if you think you may be in this position. The age of majority in most countries is eighteen however you will need to begin investigating your options at least twelve months prior to ensure the paperwork is completed in time. As a parent this will ensure your child's rights are still protected while they go about developing the skills they require in order to achieve independence (if this is possible).

TIP 73: EXPERIENCE THE LOVE OF A PET

The journey of life is sweeter when travelled with a dog. Author Unknown.

A house is never lonely where a loving dog waits. Author Unknown.

A dog is the only thing on earth that loves you more than he loves himself. Josh Billings.

When I look into the eyes of an animal I do not see an animal. I see a living being. I see a friend. I feel a soul. Anthony Douglas Williams.

When the kids were younger I swore I would never, ever get another dog. Dogs are like children: they require time and attention and I was already swamped with trying to live a happy, non-stressful life with my family which included two kids, one with special needs. Now before you assume I am a stereotypical non-dog-owner who thinks that having canines jump all over me with their saliva-laden tongues wagging is totally gross let it be known: I ABSOLUTELY LOVE DOGS.

As a child my parents refused to buy me a puppy so the moment I finished college and returned home from overseas I went straight to the pet shop and purchased a golden ball of fluff I named Madison. For the next few years Madison was my most loyal, devoted friend. Everywhere I went she went too and there was nothing nicer than coming home after a long day at work to see her thumping tail and adoring eyes.

After Madison lived for seventeen years I was convinced a dog wasn't for my current family. We had already gone through a string of non-exciting pets – goldfish, hermit crabs, love birds, rabbits and spider insects – all resulting in nothing but stress and more work for me. For some insane reason I was convinced these low-maintenance pets would be perfect for our family but in the end low-maintenance equaled low-interest from my children. Maybe they were still too young to appreciate these non-conventional pets but after a few weeks (okay it was mere days) they were bored and I was left to clean up the mess (literally!).

Then my son decided he had one wish and one wish only. It was to have a puppy right now. If he hadn't been so determined to get a dog I would have never contemplated the idea. To me getting a dog was crazy because I didn't have the time or patience to embrace bringing another member into our family, even though I knew all the positives that would come from such an addition. But once I opened myself up to the idea I could see the benefits of having a new pet: it would nurture responsibility in my children and give them more love and companionship than money could buy. Animals teach you about loyalty, about love, forgiveness and life. They are sweet, energetic and always delighted to be with you, whether you are sad or happy, having a good day or bad.

We ended up purchasing a gorgeous King Charles Cavalier named Scooter for my son's seventh birthday and I can honestly say it is the best gift we have ever given him. What I imagined would be a burden to me (yep I figured I would be the sole feeder and walker of this new pet) has ended up being my greatest decision. It's fair to say special needs children benefit greatly from a friendship with an animal who loves them unconditionally, especially if this pet is chosen to match your child's temperament and needs.

So consider opening your home to the love of a pet. It doesn't matter if it's a cat or dog, hamster or mouse. As long as it provides your child with a sense of love, companionship and responsibility it will be a good choice.

TIP 74: GIVE YOUR CHILD FREEDOM

Love in such a way that the person you love feels free. Thich Nhat Hanh.

Children need the freedom to appreciate the infinite resources of their hands, their eyes and their ears, the resources of forms, materials, sounds and colors. Loris Malagazzi

I know you probably think life would be so much easier if we wrapped our kids up in cotton wool (no chance of kidnapping! No accidents! Nothing bad could possibly happen!) But in actual fact both love and freedom are vital to the upbringing of a child.

Freedom is defined as the power or right to act, speak, or think as one wants. It is the state of being at liberty rather than in confinement or under physical restraint. We all see freedom as one of our God-given rights however for the most part parents do their best to limit the freedom of their children "for their own good." The amount of freedom we give our children is a constant source of angst and stress among parents. While we know they require freedom to flourish and grow, we also fear we haven't set appropriate boundaries for our children.

So how do we know how much freedom we should give our kids? Well I can't promise you that I have the right answer but I do believe every child requires as much freedom as is necessary to spread their wings. Children need to feel trusted, loved, respected, and nurtured to grow. They also need to understand that boundaries have been set to guide them and that laws have been made to be keep them safe (so both need to be followed rather than broken). Within these limitations they should be free to be themselves.

It's hard when you have a child with special needs because you can't necessarily offer them the same level of freedom other children their age may receive. I can't send my son alone on a bus or train or to the park with friends without coming up with a major contingency plan (right now it's just not possible) nor can I send him to a restaurant with another family without doing major research (thanks to his allergies). Fair enough he is still young and this may change in time but in all honesty he gains nothing from having me breathe down his neck.

Because there are still so many situations that require my presence (and therefore limit his sense of freedom) I had to come up with an alternative way of granting my son autonomy and independence. Thankfully this was easier said than done. When it comes to clothes I give him the freedom to buy and wear whatever he likes (unless it's a special occasion then he knows he needs to dress in his "smarter" clothes). I allow him freedom in his schedule to relax and have fun and he knows he is always free to speak his mind and use his voice (respectfully). My husband and I also grant him the freedom to form his opinions and contribute to discussions when we are making important decisions.

Now I know these examples may not seem like traditional forms of freedom but they are nonetheless important to a child's self-confidence and esteem. Freedom is found when an individual lets go of who he or she is expected to be and embraces who he or she really is inside and that is what we have allowed my son to be: his own person. The more you try to control something the more it controls you. So free yourself and your child from any unnecessary constraints and watch him bloom.

TIP 75: TEACH YOURSELF AND YOUR CHILD SOMETHING NEW

Think you already know everything you need to know then think again. Life is an endless source of interesting facts and unique bits of knowledge, waiting to be explored and discovered by you and your child. I am the first to admit I don't know everything (and I don't pretend to be a know-it-all) so as a test to see exactly how smart I am (gosh…would I pass or would I fail?) I went on the Internet. Well as it turns out there's ALOT I don't know because within ten minutes I discovered the following fun facts:

1. A crocodile cannot stick out its tongue.

2. DREAMT is the only English word that ends in "MT"

3. Our eyes are always the same size from birth but our nose and ears never stop growing.

4. A snail can sleep for three years.

5. A tiger has striped skin not just striped fur.

6. A shark is the only fish that can blink with both eyes.

7. The wedding ring goes on the left ring finger because it is the only finger with a vein that connects to the heart.

8. No word in the English language rhymes with orange, month, purple or silver.

9. Leonardo Da Vinci invented the scissors.

10. Reading about yawning will make you yawn too.

Would you be surprised if I admitted that I was totally clueless about these things before doing my research that day? Well don't be because I was indeed clueless, despite having a bachelor's degree and string of diplomas to my name. My point here is I don't want you or your family to become stagnant and afraid of learning new things.

I want to encourage you all to be students of life. Direct your children to learning by finding out what amuses their minds. Try to learn something new every day, whether it's a new word or song or hobby or fun fact. The day you stop learning is the day you stop growing and if you are not willing to learn then no one can help you. But if you are determined to learn, then do so because the capacity to learn is a gift and no one can stop you.

TIP 76: DANCE AND ENJOY MUSIC

Music speaks what cannot be expressed, soothes the mind and gives it rest, heals the heart and makes it whole, flows from heaven to the soul - Author Unknown.

Music gives soul to the universe, wings to the mind, flight to the imagination and life to everything - Plato.

Without music life would be a mistake - Friedrich Nietzsche.

Music is one of those simple pleasures in life that makes us feel relaxed and happy. We all have a favorite song we love to sing to, a favorite song that gets us up dancing, a favorite song when we are in the mood for reflecting on life and love. I want you to consider sharing this love with your child and introducing him or her to the beauty of music.

Think about all the special times in your life. There is probably a soundtrack that accompanies all these moments. All I have to hear is "Heaven" by Bryan Adams and I am instantly taken back to my wedding when I had my first dance with my new husband. Whenever I hear "American Pie" by Don McLean I can picture my mom dancing around in the kitchen, telling me as a young child all about her adventures working as a waitress in our family restaurant. When I hear "Wake Me Up" by Avicii I am transported instantly back to our island home, surrounded by all my loved ones, dancing and singing my heart out to this song. Each song signifies a different time in my life and has a powerful way of inciting my old memories to surface again.

Your child will have the same experiences with music but only if he or she is exposed to the beautiful art of music. So please do your best to introduce your child to this wonderful gift. Play your child your favorite songs and explain to him or her why they are so special. You can begin the day by playing soothing or uplifting songs, you can play them when you are travelling together in the car and sing. Sing out them loud, sing together, sing in the shower, sing whenever you can and express the joy that is sitting deep within your heart. Music touches us emotionally when words alone can't express the way we feel. Music releases us from the tyranny of conscious thought and just as medicine can heal the body music can heal our soul. Put simply good music doesn't have an expiration date so let the music play.

TIP 77: ENCOURAGE A LOVE OF READING AND BOOKS

I do believe something very magical can happen when you read a good book - J.K. Rowling.

Reading gives us someplace to go when we have to stay where we are - Mason Cooley.

A reader lives a thousand lives before he dies. The man who never reads lives only one - George R.R. Martin.

A child who reads will be an adult who thinks.

One of my favorite personal sayings is: YOU CAN'T BUY HAPPINESS BUT YOU CAN BUY BOOKS AND THAT'S KIND OF THE SAME THING. I really believe to be true – the love of books and reading has so many benefits.

These benefits include:

1.   Mental Stimulation – books help keep your brain sharp.

2.   Improves your vocabulary.

3.   Improves your concentration and focus.

4. Strengthens your memory skills.

5. Sparks your creativity.

6. Enriches your imagination.

7. It opens the world to children.

8. Helps you relax and unwind.

9. It's an inexpensive form of entertainment.

10. Gets you away from digital distractions.

I love it because books don't care if a person is young or old, healthy or sick, able-bodied or disabled. They just sit there, waiting to be opened and devoured by others, waiting to be loved and spoken about. The benefits I mentioned above can be gained by any child – even one with special needs - so do what you can to encourage a love of books and reading in your child.

You may need to be flexible in this goal – I know I have had to be. While my son and daughter are technically both good readers my son is definitely not the type to willingly pick up a book and settle down for a read. He needs reminders. He also prefers to read books off his iPad due to his fine motor issues (which makes page turning much slower than he likes). Both my children also need material they are interested in (you can discover this by going to a bookstore or library and seeing what books your child gravitates to).

Our school's homework requirement is that the children read twenty minutes a day. Would you be surprised if I told you my son literally sets a timer so that he can escape the room after twenty minutes? This has changed however since I introduced him to the concept of audiobooks. I still make him follow the pages as the speaker reads so he can visually recognize new words (so technically he is reading). However his interest and stamina is much higher when he listens to an audiobook, as opposed to when he is alone with a paperback and his thoughts.

This works for us – in your family some entirely different might work. So find a book to suit your own child. It may be a picture book or a longer story, fiction or non-fiction, on a digital device or in traditional form. You may choose read to him or alongside him, for just five minutes or five hours (except I would be envious of that - my children would probably fall asleep after an hour.) Do whatever feels right for you and your child.

TIP 78: FIND YOUR ESCAPE

When I speak about escape I should make it clear I am not referring to anything involving drugs, alcohol or an impromptu gallivant to join a travelling circus. I am talking about simple escapes, that allow you to forget about your worries and stresses for a little while.

So how do I escape? Well I make sure to book in at least one facial or massage into my schedule every month. Maybe once upon a time these were super-expensive indulgences but I have always managed to find fantastic local deals on group buying apps like Groupon. I treasure these me-time experiences because they are so pampering and relaxing. For one long hour I can blissfully empty my head, let go of everything and enjoy sixty precious minutes of heaven. For days afterwards I still feel like I am on cloud nine.

I also have my favorite TV shows that I love to watch. They include Modern Family, The Goldbergs and The Middle and we enjoy watching them together as a family. They are a temporary escape from our real everyday lives and we enjoy the laughs they provide us with. Once a year I also have an annual girls weekend away and I also make sure to schedule regular dinners and coffees with my friends so I can catch up with them and have a chance to vent, chat, giggle, and release everything that is playing on my mind. I like to read, listen to music and watch movies. I also love to Skype friends who are overseas and I make sure to schedule regular camping trips and holidays with my family so we can escape our regular routines and have a good old-fashioned break from life.

All of these activities help keep me relaxed and sane and I recommend you do the same – find the things you love to do so that you feel like you have had some form of a break. Something that allows you to return to your everyday activities with a clear head and fresh resolve to do your best to enjoy everything life has to offer.

TIP 79: APPROACH FINANCIAL CHALLENGES WITH OPEN COMMUNICATION & TEAMWORK

I think it's safe to say that having a child with special needs provides a financial strain that other families do not have to deal with. Because I have a child with special needs I am not able to go out and find any full-time job that requires me to place my child into after-school care. I didn't start working again until my son had started school and even then I searched for and was lucky enough to find a flexible job that enabled me to work a few days a week during school hours. Flexibility is a must because my son had so many important appointments that can't be rescheduled to a time that suits me best and I am grateful to have a boss that supports this need of mine. She trusts that I will always get the job done, even if I swap my days around or call in at short notice to say my child is sick and needs to urgently get to another hospital appointment.

Balancing the family budget requires you and your partner to work together as a team. It requires having common goals and having your family support these goals. Don't blame each other when the tough times hit, as casting blame never solves the problem. Decide you will find a way to tackle the problem in a way you both see fit. I'm assuming you both work hard (either inside or outside the home) so acknowledge each other's individual efforts. Sacrifices may need to be made but that's okay if in the long term this sacrifice helps you achieve your ultimate goal.

If you would like to work more but can't do so due to your child's additional needs then look at what kind of work you can do from home. There are lots of options available if you keep your eyes open. You can go back and study via correspondence if that is something you wish to do. You can also check in with a financial advisor and see if they have any useful wisdom or advice to offer. Think about what you love to do and how you can go about making money from this passion. Money is not the be-all and end-all in life but it helps immensely when the money you have is managed well.

TIP 80: COPE WITH DIVORCE

It would be presumptuous of me to assume every reader here is involved in a happy marriage. There will be some who have experienced divorce or are currently separated so I thought it would be useful to look at how divorce affects children with special needs.

Here are some things to note:

1. Divorce is traumatic for any child but perhaps more so for children with special needs as they already face enough challenges in life.

2. Divorce can cause stress and mood changes in a child and their academic performance may suffer.

3. It helps immensely if you explain clearly to your child what is happening. Be open and honest, while being conscious and respectful of their age and level of development.

4. If your child still has an active relationship with your ex-partner then do you best to encourage it!

5. Try to include your ex-partner in family celebrations and special occasions like birthdays.

6. Use a calendar to mark the days when he or she will be spending time with mommy or daddy again.

7. Facilitate other forms of communication like telephone calls so he or she can call the other parent on his or her own initiative.

8. Understand that raising a special needs child unfortunately does put an extra toll on marriages and relationships. It just does…

9. But please do let your child's disability or condition destroy or interfere any further with your relationship.

10. If you maintain a civilised relationship with your ex-partner following your breakup your child will benefit most from it.

11. An amicable split will help improve your child's self-confidence, sense of security and self-esteem.

12. A breakup should not signify a long-term war. Instead it should be the beginning of a peaceful agreement of co-parenting in two different households.

13. This is of course easier said than done. Just do your best and strive to make this happen.

14. Understand marriages can sometimes be a mistake but children never are.

15. Sometimes life doesn't turn out the way you expected it to. But that's life.

16. When you are dealt a bad hand try not to give up or feel sorry for yourself.

17. Instead pick yourself back up and start again. You won't always get it right but it helps when your heart is filled with hope and a love for life again.

TIP 81: AVOID DRAMA

If you did not see it with your own eyes or hear it with your own ears, don't invent it with your small mind and share it with your big mouth.
Author Unknown.

While it's entertaining to watch good drama on TV whenever you need an escape it's not so fun when your own life is filled with it. By drama I mean any exciting, emotional or unexpected event or circumstance that potentially threatens your sense of peace. As for the term drama queen it typically refers to individuals who consistently over-react or over-exaggerate the importance of nonthreatening events. They experience extreme emotions, constantly get snowed under one serious problem then another and seemed attached to this pattern of irrational behavior.

Do you want this type of drama in your life? No way. This isn't the fun sort of drama. This is the type that gives you a headache, that makes you want to rip out your hair or run away to a deserted island. Thankfully the drama I'm referring to doesn't just walk into your life. You either create it, invite it or associate with it. So if you already have enough on your plate by tending to a child with special needs I recommend putting an immediate stop to the silly drama, which drains you of both time and energy. Real people who value their time avoid drama because they know their time is too precious to waste. And don't start drama yourself if you say you hate drama. Some of our best decisions are often what we choose NOT to get involved with.

TIP 82: HAVE A SENSE OF HUMOR

A person without a sense of humor is like a wagon without springs. It's jolted by every pebble on the road. Henry Ward Beecher.

A sense of humor is a major defense against minor troubles. Mignon McLaughlin.

Life is so much easier when you have a sense of humor. Honestly it is. I know you may think there is absolutely nothing funny about your life as it is but that isn't what having a sense of humor is about. It means the ability to appreciate or express situations, speech and writings that are thought to be comical or amusing. You don't have to be funny yourself per se (I say this because I myself am not really funny and I tend to veer on the serious side of personalities – always have, even before having a child with special needs).

But still I am happy to laugh at myself and I can take a joke as much as I can make one. Even when things aren't going well I know how put things into perspective and have a giggle. That's because sometimes the only two choices you have are to either laugh or cry and I personally would much prefer a chuckle. I realized long ago my problems and conflicts were easier to deal with when looked upon with humor rather than rage.

Now before you decide there is absolutely nothing funny in your life I want you to look up Shane Burcaw who has a blog called *Laughing At My Nightmare*. Shane, who has muscular dystrophy, started the blog in 2011 to tell his story about living with his muscle-wasting disease.

His stories are all fun and funny and he has no issues whatever laughing at the problems he is dealing with in life. People noticed and the blog has now amassed over 500,000 followers (a number that still continues to grow every day).

Shane's goal is to show the world how laughter and humor can improve people's lives. Trust me it can improve yours too. Don't let a bad day make you feel like you have a bad life – find a way to laugh at things. Every special needs parenting survival kit should come with a sense of humor because it is the key to lightening your load of problems.

TIP 83: WRITE KIND AND THOUGHTFUL NOTES

When was the last time you wrote your child a kind and thoughtful note? Actually let's make that ANYONE a kind and thoughtful note? When the advent of all this amazing technology many people have unfortunately stopped putting pen to paper. We now write texts if we want to send someone a quick message, we use emails to do the same thing. Yet neither method delivers the same unique spark or joy that I felt as a child opening up a well-travelled envelope from a pen pal or friend.

I urge you to pull out some paper now and write your child a quick note. It doesn't have to be anything long and winded. It can simply say "I love you" or "Good Luck" or "Have a nice day." You can slip it into your child's school lunch note or leave it on his or her night stand. I have even been known scribble messages across my child's banana snack at school when I haven't had paper on hand (he has a good giggle before throwing away the banana skin).

So take the time put your thoughts and feelings down onto paper and share them with the people you love, especially your children. You have no excuses here. Most people will receive only a few notes in their entire lifetime, even though note-writing takes such little time (rarely more than a few minutes). But these notes can mean so much – they are treasured, appreciated and often read many times over. So write one today.

TIP 84: IGNORE SLIGHTS

I know it's sometimes hard to ignore slights especially when you think about what that word really means (being insulted by someone treating or speaking to you without proper respect or attention). It sucks but what sucks even more is when you let little things bother you.

Right now the world is filled with inconsiderate fools, selfish drama queens, immature twats and silly jerks. Do you want to waste your time thinking or stressing about them? Try not to read too much into the situation and don't let little things bother you. Most people are preoccupied with their own issues and are not intentionally trying to hurt or belittle you (or maybe they are and if that's the case it's time to take the higher road.)

So the next time someone ignores you or your child or keeps you waiting, remember you are in control of your actions. The best action to take in the case of slights is to put these non-important individuals out of your mind.

TIP 85: CHOOSE THE RIGHT CONFIDANTS

I know this probably sounds like a weird tip to suggest to a parent raising a special needs child but it comes from a place of care. I know what it's like to have lots of thoughts and feelings to process and it helps me immensely when I speak with other people about the things our family is going through. But there have been times in the past when I have been too open and honest with others and I regret spilling my heart with people who remained closed in return.

Your family's situation and your child's condition are personal matters – you can choose to share it with whoever you wish. So choose wisely. Choose confidantes who are understanding and trustworthy. You need to know that if you are sharing something private that they will not repeat it to others, especially if that is your wish. If people don't seem genuine or kind, loyal or trustworthy then it is fine to remain tight-lipped when it comes to questioning. Be polite and don't delve into any descriptive detail. You don't ever need to feel forced to divulge any information you don't feel comfortable sharing. It is far better to have a few trustworthy friends that you would trust with your life than a million friends that you cannot depend on to keep your private life personal.

TIP 86: MINIMISE SIBLING RIVALRY

Siblings will always fight – lucky us! But listening to them do so can be both frustrating and stressful especially when you already have an additional load on your plate. Parents however play a key role in helping to nurture good sibling relationships. We have the power to reduce sibling rivalry, which is the natural competitiveness and animosity some children have from spending a lot of time in each other's company. To reduce conflict:

1. Encourage activities that foster fun and teamwork.

2. Give your children the tools to work out conflicts in a constructive and respectful manner.

3. Do not compare your children to each other. This is the quickest way to fuel the fire of sibling rivalry.

4. Try to work out what is responsible for the conflict. Do they compete for your time and attention? Do they fight more when they are bored or tired? If you see a pattern that might explain their negative behavior then you can do your best to address or minimise the scenarios that lead to this conflict.

5. Appreciate and respect your children's differences. They will each have something special to contribute to your family.

6. If they have different interests and temperaments this may be the reason for your conflict. Look at what you can do to teach them to respect each other. Listening is one way of showing respect. Remind them how important it is to be kind to others, whether it is a stranger or family member. They should learn to treat others how they themselves wish to be treated.

7. It's okay for your children to not always agree with other but they need to learn how to disagree with each other respectfully, without hurting each other's feelings. They should not bully each other, call each other names or engage in physical fighting.

8. Emphasise what family is all about. Families stick together through thick and thin. They can have fun together. Even if your children prefer to spend their time with outside friends now in the future their family will become more important to them. Whether we like it or not, we can't escape our family and most of us have an unshakable bond with our siblings that is hard to shake or match.

TIP 87: DON'T JUDGE OTHERS

Who are you to judge the life I live? I know I'm not perfect, and I don't live to be, but before you start pointing fingers...make sure your hands are clean! – Bob Marley.

We tend to judge others by their behavior and ourselves by our intentions. – Albert Schlieder.

There are wounds that never show on the body that are deeper and more hurtful than anything that bleeds. – Laurell K. Hamilton

Before you judge me, make sure you're perfect. – Clint Eastwood.

If we could look into each other's hearts and understand the unique challenges each of us faces, I think we would treat each other much more gently, with more love, patience, tolerance, and care. Marvin J. Ashton.

This is such a simple tip but so important: DON'T JUDGE. Yes even if others are wasting every single of their day judging you I want you to refrain from behaving in a similarly negative manner. You don't like it when others judge you, so do you best to not judge others. The term judgmental refers to someone who forms a lot of harsh and critical opinions about other people without reason. They tend to make grand-sweeping statements in a negative light and are rarely open-minded and easy-going.

196

Let me tell you one truth: judging a person doesn't define who they are; it defines who you are. I've said it before and I will say it again: nobody is perfect and everyone has their issues. You will never, ever know what other people are going through because everybody is fighting their own unique war in life just like you.

So before you judge others – their life, their past or their characters, think about the fact you have not walked in their shoes, just as they have not walked in yours. You have not lived their sorrow, their pain, their ups or downs, their doubts or fears. Everyone has their own story to tell so unless you have lived every single experience alongside them (and news alert – you haven't) think twice before you make negative judgements about others. Counting other people's sins does not make you a saint. As Mother Teresa so wisely said, "If you judge people then you have no time to love them."

TIP 88: BE TIDY

Have nothing in your houses that you do not know to be useful or to be beautiful. – William Morris.

Think this is a crazy parenting tip then think again. A tidy house usually means a clear and clutter-free mind. Now I know I am far from being the tidiest person in the world – whenever we are busy mess tends to accumulate quite quickly in our home. The ironing pile grows huge, clothes and crap get left in places where they simply do not belong and our home just gets UNTIDY.

Let me tell you how this messiness makes me feel. It makes me feel crap. I hate it. I can't think straight and I get irritable for no reason. Then when the house finally gets cleaned and everything is returned to its rightful home I feel the weight of chaos lift from me. I feel clear, free and at peace. For some crazy reason I parent better when the house is organized and tidy. I make better decisions and don't feel pulled in all directions, because the confusion and disarray that mess brings is now gone.

If you aren't convinced that having a tidy house will help you immensely in your role as a parent, test it out. If it fails all you have gained in the process is a more organized home. If it works, then devise a way to keep your living environment looking great on a regular basis.

Some tips to help you:

1. Do it now. If you see something that needs to be put away pick it up and put it away. If the mirrors need a spray then spray them; if your basins need a wipe down then wipe them today.

2. Start with the easy stuff. Now is not the time to begin going through old photo albums. But if your wardrobes are a mess and you also happen to wear clothes every day (guessing you do) then feel free to tend to it.

3. Throw away everything you don't love or need. If it doesn't bring you joy or it isn't useful now is the time to bin it.

4. Stop accumulating STUFF. The more possessions you own the greater the chance your house will be messy simply because there is only a finite amount of space in your house.

5. Make your bed every day – it's the one thing you can do to instantly make your bedrooms look neater and it takes only a few minutes of your time.

6. Work in 15 minutes bursts. It's hard to commit to a whole day of cleaning but pretty easy and possible to commit to a daily 15 minute workout. Think you can't do a lot in 15 minutes then think again. You can clean a toilet in that time, vacuum a few rooms, fold a basket or two of washing.

7. Delegate responsibilities – yes it's fine to ask your children or partner to help you with tasks they are capable of doing.

8. Keep your cleaning supplies in one place and on hand. I have mine in a caddy so it's easy to grab whenever I need to clean something quickly.

9. Be consistent. Unfortunately your house will only stay tidy if you look after it on a regular basis.

10. Have a philosophy about tidiness. Your house doesn't have to be perfect but it does help if everyone in your family understands there is "a place for everything and everything in its place". Or that they shouldn't put things down "just for now" – I say put it back where it belongs.

TIP 89: ADMIT WHEN YOU ARE WRONG

I have long since learned as all should learn, not to make excuses when wrong. Just admit it and try to profit from it. – Jesse Livermore.

There is no better test of a man's integrity than his behavior when he is wrong. – Marvin Williams.

Yep it's hard being a parent because our kids assume that simply because we are older we must be wiser and never get things wrong. Ah...all I can say is I wish. I'm still human and yep I do make mistakes...on a regular basis. My advice to you is if you are in the wrong, own up to what you didn't do right. If you are wrong, say you are wrong. Don't make excuses. This is the quickest way to earn your child's respect. Admitting you are wrong is an act of strength. Your child looks to you as a guide and he will appreciate both your courage and your honesty.

TIP 90: NEVER ASSUME

Assumptions are the termites of relationships. – Henry Winkler.

Don't make assumptions. Find the courage to ask questions and to express what you really want. Communicate with others as clearly as you can to avoid misunderstandings, sadness and drama. With just this one agreement you can completely transform your life. – Miguel Angel Ruiz.

It's hard when your child has a disability because people often make assumptions about your child's potential based on a label. Maybe they assume just because your child may not be able to walk or talk that he is intellectually impaired. Or maybe if your child does have an intellectual or cognitive impairment they assume he doesn't have thoughts or feelings, a heart or any deep substance.

It sucks I know because I have experienced this myself. But we are in the privileged position of being able to break down those stereotypes and educate others as to what disabilities are all about. As the slogan goes we should label jars, not people.

WE CAN TEACH OTHERS:

1. That a disability does not define who a person is as an individual. Individuals with disabilities are people first.

2. People with disabilities aren't always brave, inspirational or courageous simply because they have a condition they live with. They are often scared or worried too.

3. People with disabilities aren't constantly sick or in pain. "Normal" people get sick too and people with disabilities aren't always suffering or experiencing pain due to their condition.

4. People with disabilities aren't special just because they have a condition. They do not always need to be accommodated nor should they be underestimated.

5. People with disabilities do not deserve our pity. Having a disability isn't a tragedy. It doesn't always signify a poor quality of life either. This is simply an assumption.

6. People with disabilities don't always need our help. Sure some may have difficulty doing things and may require our assistance but this does not mean they are dependent on help.

7. They also don't just want to associate with others with disabilities. They want to associate with all sorts of folk.

8. People with disabilities can lead full and productive lives. They can be happy, positive and satisfied. They can be just as capable of participating in the community as people without disabilities.

9. Never make assumptions. It is far better to ask questions. If you do you just may learn something new.

TIP 91: RESPECT YOUR CHILD'S INDIVIDUALITY

Today you are you, that is truer than true. There is no one alive who is youer than You! - Dr. Seuss.

If a man is not faithful to his own individuality, he cannot be loyal to anything. - Claude McKay.

You laugh because I am different. I laugh because you are all the same. - Unknown.

I think it is important to teach our children with special needs to take pride in whatever it is that makes them different. Individuality is what divides a person from the rest of the crowd. Your child cannot be duplicated or replaced – their individuality is what makes them so special and I think that is such a great thing. There is no point in being the same as everyone else. So encourage your child to shine and embrace their individuality. Teach him or her to respect it, be proud of it and own it. As they say: stop trying to fit in, when you were born to stand out. (Gosh I love that!)

TIP 92: MINIMISE CONFLICT

Peace is not the absence of conflict but the ability to cope with it. – Dorothy Thomas.

I don't know a single person in life that doesn't have conflict. – Joaquin Phoenix.

Do you really need more conflict and stress in life? I'm guessing no. I'm guessing that like me you would love to live a fulfilling and peaceful existence with your family and others, without needless conflict impacting your life.

Here are some tips to help you minimize the presence of conflict:

1. Remember dialogue is the most effective method of resolving conflict.

2. Conflict cannot continue without your participation so step away.

3. As Max Lucado said conflict is inevitable but combat is optional.

4. Identify the problem – it helps if you know and recognise the issues that keep propping up in your life.

5. Brainstorm solutions. Try to be as creative as possible regarding what you can do to say goodbye to or minimise conflict.

6. The goal is to find a win-win approach.

Since children have different needs and preferences you have to understand that some conflict is unavoidable. But you can teach them that life isn't a competition. You never, ever ultimately win if you get your way by using force or avoiding a problem. Our aim in life is usually to live a peaceful, happy life and you cannot achieve that if it is filled with conflict, drama, jealously, anger, unhealthy competition and rivalries. So ditch the drama and all the unnecessary baggage and begin living your conflict-free life today.

TIP 93: DO NOT SET YOUR CHILD UP FOR FAILURE

Failure is only an opportunity to begin again. Only this time more wisely. – Henry Ford.

I know we don't do this on purpose but there are times when parents with special needs unintentionally set their child up for failure. Maybe we expect our child to be more social than they are capable of being. Or maybe we expect them to do a task within a set timeframe and they simply move at a slower pace (something I have been guilty of in the past). Whatever it is I want you to realize that if you do this on a regular basis it can potential damage your child's self-esteem. Just as I would never ask you to translate my book into another language that you are not familiar with (wouldn't that be fun!) we should be mindful of the things we ask of our children too.

Try to give your child tasks he or she is capable of managing or if you are attempting to introduce something new – do it slowly and at their pace. This is how we build our children's self-esteem and make them feel confident enough to try new things. Admittedly failures are a part of life. If you don't fail you don't learn and if you don't learn you never change. But it will help our children immensely if you don't set your child up for failure time and time again.

TIP 94: ACKNOWLEDGE YOUR CHILD'S EMOTIONS

Your child is human so he or she is going to feel a vast range of emotions in his or her life. Some of these emotions include:

- Happiness
- Sadness
- Uncomfortable
- Overwhelmed
- Eagerness
- Confident
- Jealous
- Embarrassed
- Concerned
- Confused
- Loved
- Loving
- Tired
- Anxious
- Envy
- Scared
- Hopeful
- Content
- Capable
- Inspired
- Guilty
- Frustrated
- Grateful
- Cautious

And so on and so on and so on.

Have you ever felt any of these emotions? I'm sure you have so I want you to acknowledge that it is fine for your child to feel these emotions too. There is no reason to get angry when he is feeling angry, to feel frustrated when he is feeling frustrated or upset when he is upset. Accept that feeling these emotions is a necessary part of life and there is nothing worse than when a person tells you "you can't" or "you shouldn't" feel a particular way.

Give your child permission to feel what he feels and if his emotions are weighing him down provide him with the tools to manage his negative emotions. Managing your emotions is the key; pretending they do not exist or ignoring them is not.

TIP 95: MANAGE MELT-DOWNS

Even though my son does not have a condition that is characterized by regular meltdowns I know there are lots of children with special needs who do have them and that it causes their parents much heartache and stress. No one likes to see their child upset. That being said sometimes kids who need the most love will ask for it in what some may consider an "unloving" way. From my own experience I believe that children who have meltdowns do so because they haven't yet a) learned how to properly manage, b) they have run out of tools to use to regulate their feelings in a new situation or event. Or c) they have found in the past their meltdown was successful in getting them what they want (perhaps it was exiting a situation or receiving their parent's attention) so they try it again.

Meltdowns can be difficult to manage when they happen with greater frequency and intensity but there are some things you can do to try and control the situation. The first is recognizing the triggers – if you know your child is affected by particular noises or smells, textures or lights then it is best to try and manage the sort of situations your child is placed in if possible.

Pay attention to cues – what is your child trying to tell you? It helps if you are responsive and sensitive to the needs of your child. Just like I need to be super-vigilant of my child's safety due to his mobility issues you too may need to be hyper-aware of instances that could trigger your child. If he is tired or acting aggressive or has eaten something which he may be sensitive to be mindful of this. Take steps to prevent the beginning of a meltdown by removing potential triggers.

Also I don't want you to worry what other people think if your child "loses it" over what seems like a silly thing. Their thoughts or opinions don't matter! Just do whatever you can calm your child down or divert his attention. You know your child best – you know and understand their condition. It will be okay, I promise.

TIP 96: HAVE FAITH

Hope is putting faith to work when doubting would be easier.
Thomas S. Monson

Faith is taking the first step even when you don't see the whole stair case.
Martin Luther King Jr.

I have waited until now to broach the idea of faith in this book because I understand my readers will all have different beliefs and come from different religious backgrounds. I myself was raised a Catholic but I am open to embracing all religions that give individuals a sense of belonging, hope and faith.

To me the idea of something greater existing makes me feel at peace. It comforts me during my times of need and I am grateful for the words that reassure me when I feel as if the world is simply too overwhelming to conquer on my own. Even if your spiritual connection is different from mine please accept that it's okay. We are all entitled to our own beliefs and no matter which God or greater being we choose to follow the choice is a good one if the words and beliefs resonate with us and give us a sense of peace.

Faith is all about believing. It is about having hope in a world that can potentially be quite dark and scary. Let your faith be bigger than your fears. You don't know how your life will unfold but you do know that whatever happens will usually be the right outcome for now.

So be patient and trust that better things are coming because there isn't enough room in your mind for both worry and faith. You ultimately must decide which you want living there – faith or worry? Which will make you feel happier and at peace?

Having faith is about not giving up. So don't be afraid, surrender to what is and have faith in what will be. Having faith is about seeing light with your heart when all your eyes see is darkness. It's about understanding that everything will come to you at the right moment. Just breathe and find comfort in the notion that having faith will get you through your darker days.

TIP 97: ENJOY NATURE AND EVERYTHING THE WORLD HAS TO OFFER

The earth has music for those who listen. Shakespeare.

There is a pleasure in the pathless woods, there is rapture on the lonely shore, there is society, where none intrudes, by the deep sea, and music in its roar: I love not man the less, but nature more. Lord Byron.

In every walk with nature one receives far more than he seeks. John Muir.

Most of us find our lives follow a predictable pattern. We wake up, send our kids to school or maybe prepare for the day with our children by our sides; we go to work and run errands and do our best to keep our homes in order. All in all the bulk of our hours are spent inside four closed walls. This is comforting to some because it's a wonderful feeling when we have created a safe haven which we call home. At the same time this lifestyle robs us of the opportunity to spend time outdoors, experiencing the real world.

The world is more than what you see on daily basis, day in and day out, week after week, year after year. It is more than the room with the TV, it is more than your office space; it is more than your kitchen or the inside of your car. Outside suburbia there is a whole world waiting to be discovered: beaches and rivers, forests and mountains, lakes and wilderness.

I encourage you to sometimes get lost in nature. Know that the whole world is yours to explore. Go outside looking and you may be surprised what you may find there. Oftentimes it is in nature that I have found myself, my voice, my open heart. Sure there is no WIFI in the forest or at the beach but I promise, you will find there a different sort of connection with the world.

Beautiful things like the trees and ocean and flowers don't ask for attention but they are there, waiting for you to find them and enjoy their existence. I have personally never found time spent amongst nature to be a waste of time. Introduce your child to this beauty. I understand they may be limited in their capacity to enjoy different forms of nature (for example my son is never going to be able to climb a steep mountain or even a fairly little one) but there will be some way they can enjoy it in a means that best suits them.

Maybe you can dip your child's toes into an ocean, maybe she can breathe in the perfume of field filled with flowers; maybe he can enjoy the solitude of the forest just by sitting under a tree. Whichever way works for you think about introducing this amazing world to your child, a world that is so much greater than any of us, a world that existed way before any of us ever graced this planet and which will continue to exist long after we are gone.

TIP 98: LIVE IN THE MOMENT

Living in the moment is being aware of the moment we are in. If our minds are in the past or future we are not truly alive in the present. Satsuki Shibuya.

He said, "There are only two days in the year that nothing can be done. One is called yesterday and the other is called tomorrow, so today is the right day to love, believe, do and mostly live." Dalai Lama.

Give every day the chance to become the most beautiful of your life. Mark Twain.

The purpose of life, after all, is to live it, to taste experience to the utmost, to reach out eagerly and without fear for newer and richer experience. Eleanor Roosevelt.

If there is one tip I think will help you cope better it's this one: live in the moment and don't think too much or too hard about all the things awaiting you in the future.

Honestly sometimes we need to stop analyzing the past, stop planning the future, stop figuring out exactly how we feel, stop deciding what we want and just see what happens. Don't think about what can happen in a month.

Don't think about what can happen in a year. Just focus on the 24 hours in front of you and do what you can to get closer to where you want to be.

Here's the hard truth: you don't get to experience the same moment twice in life. You don't get to do this day over. Seriously you don't. When you wake up tomorrow this day we are experiencing right now will be all gone, done and dusted. It's up to you to see the beauty of everyday things. So be here right now - enjoy life today and by today I mean right this very second, this very moment. Don't wish away days or wait for better ones to come because honestly you don't know what's around the corner, none of us do.

All we have is NOW. So I want you to stop and enjoy the present right now while it is happening. Before it's too late, before you realize that maybe - just maybe - it was always fine, fun, fulfilling and enough.

TIP 99: EVERYTHING WILL BE OKAY

In three words I can sum up everything I've learned about life: it goes on.

R. Frost.

Let it be known right now:

You will have good days.
And you will have bad days.
If you fall down
Pick yourself back up.
If the wind blows in ways you didn't expect
Adjust your sails.
Not everything will be okay all the time
But some things will.
The more you know and trust yourself
The less you will allow things to upset you.
Tough times don't last
But tough people do.
Sometimes the darkest nights
Produce the brightest stars.
Knowing this will keep you strong.
Because everything will be okay in the end
And if it's not okay, it's not the end.

TIP 100: DO NOT CONSIDER THIS BOOK THE BE-ALL AND END-ALL IN SPECIAL NEEDS PARENTING – TAKE THE TIME TO DO YOUR OWN RESEARCH

Life is either a daring adventure or nothing at all. -Helen Keller

I would have loved it if this book covered every single battle and challenge that a parent faces while parenting a child with special needs. I would have loved it if within these pages you found the answers to all your questions and it ultimately stopped you from having to look any further. However I am not naïve or over-ambitious in that way – I know this book is just one tool out of many that a parent may or may not choose to keep in his or her artillery for use in daily life.

I have a son with a physical disability so a lot of my advice comes from having this experience. Everywhere I go in life I see the challenges that could potentially impact a mobility-impaired individual – the stairs leading up to a place that everyone is desperate to visit, the tight aisles and spaces within shops and restaurants, all the beautiful countries and islands in this world that haven't even begun to accommodate physically disabled individuals – places that I have gone to myself and that I wish I could share with him too.

Here's the thing though. Even if your own child can walk and talk just fine but instead struggles socially, cognitively, behaviorally or physically in a different way I understand. Sure maybe I don't fully comprehend your own unique situation or diagnosis but I understand what it's like to have a child who is "different" from the norm. I understand how desperately you want your child to live a fulfilling life. I understand the heartache, the stress and the joys that might not seem so joyful to outsiders but to us it feels like the most incredible feeling on earth.

If I haven't provided you here with enough information or advice relevant to your own personal situation then I am encouraging you to seek it. Do your research, keep asking questions and don't give up until you find an answer that helps you and your child's situation. We are so lucky to live in a world right now which is almost bursting with information. So if I have missed something important please keep looking until you find the right words and advice to help put your mind at ease. I want nothing more than for you and your family to live a life blessed with peace and happiness.

BONUS TIP 101: SEEK ENCOURAGEMENT FROM OTHERS WHO HAVE PROSPERED DESPITE ALL ODDS

While it's a great achievement for any person to perform an extraordinary act, when it's done by someone with a debilitating disability it redefines the term "awe-inspiring" for me. Here is a list of my favorite individuals who have made a major mark on society through their actions or succeeded despite all odds.

Hellen Keller; 1880 – 1968 Diagnosis: Blind and Deaf

One of the most inspiring stories of an individual who managed to succeed despite all odds is Helen Keller, who overcame the adversity of being deaf and blind to become one of the leading humanitarians of the 20th century. Born physically normal Keller lost her sight and hearing at the age of 19 months, leaving her to live in a world that seemed totally isolated. However through the instruction of a remarkable teacher named Anne Sullivan as a little girl Helen Keller learned to understand and communicate with the world around her. Keller learned from Sullivan to read and write in Braille and to use the hand signals of the deaf-mute, which she could understand only by touch.

Keller grew up to be a prolific author and campaigned heavily for women's and workers' rights, and socialism, as well as many other progressive causes. Widely honored throughout the world, she founded the American Civil Liberties Union (ACLU) and traveled to over 39 countries, meeting every US President from Grover Cleveland to Lyndon B. Johnson.

She also became friends with many famous figures, including Charlie Chaplin, Alexander Graham Bell and Mark Twain. Through her amazing work Helen was able to alter the world's perception of the capabilities of the handicapped and show others how courage, intelligence and dedication can help strength the human spirit to overcome adversity.

Stephen Hawking Born 1942 Diagnosis: ALS

At the age of 21 Stephen Hawking was diagnosed with a rare early-onset slow-progressing form of ALS (amyotrophic lateral sclerosis) also known as motor neurone disease. At the time doctors gave him a life expectancy of two years however he has since lived for more than 40 years with the disease, that has left him unable to walk, talk, breathe easily, swallow or hold his up head without difficulty. At the time he was told he was not a remarkable college student (he received mediocre grades in middle school) but despite this assessment he has become an internationally renowned Physicist, cosmologist, author, professor and Director of Research at the Centre for Theoretical Cosmology within the University of Cambridge. His book *A Brief History of Time* stayed on the British Sunday Times bestseller list for a record-breaking 237 weeks. In spite of being wheelchair bound and dependent on a computerised voice system for communication Hawking continues to live an abundant life with his family (he has three children and three grandchildren) while also traveling and lecturing extensively on theoretical physics.

Nick Vujicic Born 1982 Diagnosis: Tetra-Amelia Syndrome

I have a serious soft spot for Nick as he was born in Australia like me and I discovered him (one of his early lectures specifically) long before he became a world renowned motivational speaker. As soon as I heard him speak, even though he was still young at the time, I knew he held the power to positively impact others, especially physically-challenged individuals who may have felt depressed or confronted by their limitations.

Vujicic was born with tetra-amelia syndrome, a rare disorder characterized by the absence of all four limbs (he does however have two toes on one small foot). As a child he struggled not only physically but emotionally yet eventually he came to terms with his disability and at the age of seventeen he started his own not-for-profit organization called Life without Limbs. During secondary school Vujicic was elected school captain and at age twenty one he graduated from Griffith University with a double major in Accounting and Financial Planning. He now travels as a motivational speaker, is the author of numerous books including *Your Life Without Limits* and happily married with two children. In his words:

Dream big my friend and never give up. We all make mistakes but none of them are mistakes. Take one day at a time. Embrace the positive attitudes, perspectives, principles and truths I share, and you too will overcome.

Rick Hoyt Born 1962 Diagnosis: Cerebral Palsy

Another favourite inspirational person of mine – I first saw the Hoyts on an Oprah show back when I was still a teenager (long before I had any special needs children of my own). When I saw Rick Hoyt with his father Dick I was instantly spellbound by the love and dedication this father had for his son. At birth Rick was diagnosed with severe cerebral palsy and the doctors were blunt. They said "forget about Rick, put him away, put him in an institution, he's going to be a vegetable for the rest of his life." Institutionalising their child was however never an option for his parents and they decided to raise Rick just like his two brothers.

At the age of 11 Rick was fitted with a computer that enabled him to communicate. With this communication device, Rick was also able to attend public schools for the first time. Rick went on to graduate from Boston University in 1993 with a degree in special education and later worked at Boston College in a computer lab helping to develop systems to aid in communication and other tasks for people with disabilities.

Team Hoyt was formed in 1997 after Rick asked his father Dick if they could run in a race together to benefit a lacrosse player at his school who had become paralysed.

They have since competed in over a thousand endurance events, including marathons, triathlons and Ironman competitions with Dick pushing his son in a custom-made running chair. They have also run the Boston Marathon 32 times and in 1992 Team Hoyt biked and ran across the United States, completing a full 3,735 miles in 45 days. This astonishing feat of love and courage was sparked after Rick told his father after their first event "Dad when I'm running, it feels like I'm not handicapped." Running together became a way to send a message to the world that "everybody should be included in everyday life." Such is the power of a parent's love!

Mary Temple Grandin 1947: Diagnosis: Autism

Mary Temple Grandin is not only an American professor at animal science at Colorado State University she is also a best-selling author, autism activist and consultant to the livestock industry on animal behavior. In 2010 she was named by Time 100 as one of the one hundred most influential people in the world and is the subject of the award-winning biographical film, Temple Grandin. She also invented the "hug box", a device designed to calm those on the autism spectrum. Her message to the world: *The world needs different kinds of minds to work together. See the person not the label. Autism is a part of who I am. I am different, but not less.*

Christy Brown, 1932 –1981, Diagnosis: Cerebral Palsy

Christy Brown was an Irish author, painter and poet who had severe cerebral palsy. Born in Dublin, he was one of 13 surviving children (out of 22 born) in a Catholic family. He was severely disabled by cerebral palsy and incapable for years of deliberate movement or speech. Doctors considered him to be intellectually disabled as well however his mother continued to speak to him, work with him, and try to teach him.

One day, he famously snatched a piece of chalk from his sister with his left foot to make a mark on a slate. At the time, only his left foot responded to his will and using his foot he was able to communicate for the first time. He is most famous for his autobiography *My Left Foot*, which was later made into an Academy Award-winning film of the same name.

Franklin Roosevelt – Born 1882-1945 Diagnosis: Paralysis

Roosevelt was the 32nd President of the United States and in 1921 contracted an illness (at the time believed to be poliomyelitis) that left him with total and permanent paralysis from the waist down. Due to fear of what the public would think the news of his disability was kept secret for numerous years and Roosevelt continued to serve his nation in an honourable and memorable way. He tried a wide range of therapies, including hydrotherapy and being fitted with iron braces. In private he used a wheelchair and despite his paralysis he retained his humor and charisma, and was elected President an unprecedented four times.

Robert Hensel Born 1969 Diagnosis: Spina Bifida

As an international poet and writer, Hensel has never let his disability come in the way of his artistic mind. "THERE WERE MANY TIMES THAT MY SCHOOLMATES WOULD LAUGH AT ME AND CALL ME NAMES SIMPLY BECAUSE OF THEIR LACK OF UNDERSTANDING OF WHY I WAS A LITTLE DIFFERENT". He was awarded the title of one of the best poets of the 20th century with over 900 publications worldwide and detains the world record at Guinness and Ripley's for the longest nonstop wheelie in a wheelchair, covering a total distance of 6.178 miles. Hensel is a leading figure within the disability community, advocating for the right and treatment of all individuals living with disabilities across the world.

Ruth Sienkiewicz-Mercer Born 1950-1998 Diagnosis: Quadriplegic

Ruth was a quadriplegic and an American disability rights activist, best known for her autobiography *I Raise My Eyes to Say Yes*, co-authored with Steven B. Kaplan. Born a healthy baby she was afflicted with a severe bout of encephalitis at the age of five weeks. At thirteen months, she was diagnosed with cerebral palsy resulting from the encephalitis and consequently her control over her entire body, except for her face and digestive system, was severely impaired.

Due to her inability to communicate normally, she was diagnosed as an imbecile at the age of five and as a teenager was sent to an institution for the mentally and physically disabled where she was severely mistreated for eight years. In 1978 she and some fellow patients were moved into their own apartment and soon after she married and published her autobiography to critical acclaim. Despite never speaking a word or having the ability to walk or feed herself she changed many people with her words and became a world renowned disability rights activist.

Ralph Braun Born 1940-2013 Diagnosis: Muscular Dystrophy

Ralph Braun was the late founder and CEO of the Braun Corporation, which is today one of the leading manufacturers of wheelchairs and accessible vehicles. At age six Braun was diagnosed with muscular dystrophy and doctors told his parents he would never be independent. Ralph and his parents were however determined to prove them wrong.

In the next few years Braun lost his ability to walk and he sent his mind to engineering the first battery-powered scooter. During his teen years he created various motorized vehicles to help him get around and by 1991 he had created the first wheelchair accessible minivan. Named the "Champion of Change" by President Barrack Obama his personal drive to keep him independent evolved into BraunAbility, the leading manufacturer of mobility products across the world. He passed away at the age of 73 but not before he made a serious impact helping launch the mobility movement.

224

Chris Burke Born 1956. Diagnosis: Down Syndrome

Chris Burke is an American actor who is best known for his character Charles "Corky" Thatcher on the television series *Life Goes On*. When Chris born his parents were told to institutionalise him but instead they decided to raise him at home and nurture his talents. He was encouraged by his supportive family to follow his dreams of being on TV and Chris became the first person with Down syndrome to star in a weekly television series. He has since appeared on numerous TV shows and movies and currently serves as the National Down Syndrome Society (NDSS) Ambassador. Chris had the faith in his own abilities and the courage to face prejudice as he pursued his dream to become an actor.

Other Memorable mentions:

Albert Einstein, Amadeus Mozart and Michelangelo

These three incredible men are all widely believed to have been on the autism spectrum. Einstein was very intelligent but had difficulty with social interactions and learning in school. Mozart was an accomplished musician from the age of five and exhibited much of the narrow focus often found in autistic individuals. Michelangelo on the other hand had an inability to form long-term attachments and other eccentricities which are easily explained by a diagnosis of autism. All three men grew to be known as world-renowned geniuses in the academic and artistic field.

Sir Isaac Newton

According to experts Newton showed many signs of having Asperger's Syndrome. He hardly spoke, had few friends and was so engrossed in his work he often forgot to eat. If nobody turned up to his lectures, he gave them anyway, talking to an empty room. He demonstrated an obsessive single-mindedness that is commonly associated with Asperger's. Newton is now widely recognized as one of the most influential scientists of all time and a key figure in the scientific revolution.

Terry Fox

Terry ran halfway across Canada with only one leg (and a prosthetic). His disability affected his ability to run across the second largest country in the world but he did it anyway.

Willie Boular

This man from Kansas was blind, mute, and had both legs amputated but he still once built a 46000 brick-sidewalk in less than 8 hours.

Steady Eddie

An Australian comedian and actor with Cerebral palsy who used his disability as the basis for his comedy. He was rewarded with a Young Australian Achievers Award and has since toured the UK, Canada and USA, releasing a big-selling album and video and winning various awards for his comedic efforts.

Marla Runyan

At the age of nine, Marla developed Stargardt's Disease, which is a form of macular degeneration that left her legally blind. Marla Runyan went on to become a three time national champion in the women's 5000 meters. She won four gold medals in the 1992 summer Paralympics. In the 1996 Paralympics she won silver in the shot put and gold in the Pentathlon. In 2000 she became the first legally blind Paralympian to compete in the Olympic Games in Sydney and a year later she co-wrote and published her autobiography *'No Finish Line: My Life As I See It.'*

Marlee Matlin

This Academy Award winning actress has been deaf since 18 months old due to a genetically malformed cochlea. Her work in film and television has resulted in four Emmy nominations, one Golden Globe Award and two additional Golden Globe nominations. She is also a prominent member of the National Association of the Deaf.

Daniel Tammet

Born in 1979 Tammet has written three incredible books based on his personal experience with Asperger Syndrome. In 2005 a UK documentary called "The Boy with the Incredible Brain" was based on his life.

Ray Charles and Stevie Wonder

These men may not have been able to see but by gosh could they sing.

Dr. Janice Brunstrom

She is the only paediatric neurologist in the U.S. who also has Cerebral Palsy, and she is one of the leading scientists in CP research. She founded the only comprehensive paediatric CP Center in the country and her main cause is correcting common misconceptions about cerebral palsy such as: *Cerebral palsy is hopeless; Cerebral palsy means low intelligence; Children with cerebral palsy do not need to stand and physicians cannot do anything about these children's vision problems.*

Itzhak Perlman

An Israeli-American conductor, pedagogue and one of the most distinguished violinists of the late 20th century. Perlman contracted polio at the age of four and today he gets around with the use of a wheelchair or the aid of crutches. He plays the violin while seated and critics say there is something so transcending about the emotions Itzhak is able to communicate through playing of his music.

Jhamak Ghimire

A poet and writer from Nepal, Jhamak has won many awards for her writing of literature. Born in 1980 with cerebral palsy, Ghimire's desire led her to learn to read and write. She went on to become one of the leading and well respected literary figures of Nepal and has also become a symbol of courage to people with disabilities around the world.

Hermann of Reichenau

Also called Herman the Cripple, he was an 11th century scholar, composer, music theorist, mathematician, and astronomer. Born with a cleft palate, cerebral palsy and also said to have spina bifida, Hermann was crippled by a paralytic disease from early childhood. At seven he was placed in a monastery by his parents who could no longer look after him and he eventually grew up to be literate in several languages and a famed religious poet and historian.

Christopher Nolan

This famed Irish author was born with cerebral palsy, after been deprived of oxygen for two hours at birth. He could only move his head and eyes but his mother believed he could understand what was going on and so used to teach him at home. Eventually they discovered a drug that allowed him to move one muscle in his neck so they attached a special pointer device to his forehead which enabled his mother to help him to type. He communicated with others solely by moving his eyes, using a signal system.

At fifteen his first book Dam-Burst of Dreams was accepted for publication and he was later awarded an Honorary Doctorate of Letter in the UK and a medal of excellence from the United Nations Society of Writers. Nolan has never spoken or signed a word in his life, yet his poetry has been compared to that of Joyce, Keats, and Yeats.